EVERLASTING
LOVE

About the Authors

As a medium, lecturer, teacher, and published author, Patrick Mathews has helped countless people around the world with his gift of communicating with those who have crossed over to the other side. His acute heightened level of connection with spirit, along with his personality and heartfelt compassion, makes him one of the most nationally known and sought-after mediums today. Patrick has appeared on numerous television shows airing on ABC, CBS, PBS, as well as many radio shows around the country, including the *Ryan Seacrest Show*. Patrick was also a featured medium on the hit television shows *Most Haunted* and *Most Haunted Live*, which were seen worldwide! Visit Mathews online at www.PatrickMathews.com.

Kathleen Mathews is an expert on Spirituality and the Afterlife. She has participated in and studied many of the readings given by her brother Patrick Mathews. Both she and her brother enjoy holding live events throughout the country and have a profound impact for those who attend. Kathy has appeared on numerous television shows airing on ABC, CBS, PBS as well as many radio shows around the country including the *Ryan Seacrest Show*. Visit Kathleen on line at www.KathyMathews.com.

EVERLASTING
LOVE

Finding Comfort Through
Communicating with Your Beloved in Spirit

PATRICK MATHEWS
KATHLEEN MATHEWS

Llewellyn Publications
Woodbury, Minnesota

FIRST EDITION
First Printing, 2014

Book design by Bob Gaul
Cover design by Ellen Lawson
Cover image: iStockphoto.com/14179300/©Wiktory
Editing by Connie Hill

Llewellyn Publications is a registered trademark of Llewellyn Worldwide Ltd.

Library of Congress Cataloging-in-Publication Data
Mathews, Patrick,
  Everlasting love: finding comfort through communicating with your beloved in spirit/Patrick Mathews, author of the bestselling *Never Say Goodbye*, with Kathleen Mathews.—First Edition.
    pages   cm
  ISBN 978-0-7387-4157-4
1. Marriage and spiritualism. 2. Love—Miscellanea. I. Title.
  BF1275.M3M38 2014
  133.9'1—dc23
                    2014029583

Llewellyn Publications
A Division of Llewellyn Worldwide Ltd.
2143 Wooddale Drive
Woodbury, MN 55125-2989
www.llewellyn.com

Printed in the United States of America

Contents

Dedication

We would like to dedicate this book to two people whose life was a wonderful love story that served as a great example to us as to what true love is —our parents.

Florence Mathews and James Mathews lived a true love story...and continue to do so.

—Patrick and Kathleen Mathews

Love

noun \'ləv\

: a feeling of strong or constant affection for a person

: attraction that includes sexual desire

: the strong affection felt by people who have a
  romantic relationship

: a person you love in a romantic way

verb \'ləv\

: to feel great affection for (someone)

: to feel love for (someone)

: to feel sexual or romantic love for (someone)

: to like or desire (something) very much

: to take great pleasure in (something)

—*Source: Merriam-Webster Dictionary*

Introduction

I wanted to join Patrick in writing this book to give you my perspective as a witness to the fantastic path we have chosen for our life's work and the wonderful stories of love that we have experienced. Patrick's voice will resonate in italics throughout the book to distinguish between the two of us.

Through our life's journey and our work, Patrick and I have done some outstanding things and have met many amazing people. Not only when by his side during readings, but also when we are conducting lectures, teaching workshops as well as being interviewed in the media, people have told us we make a great team, and I could not agree with them more. It has been a blessing to be at Patrick's side, and we know our work helps so many with the passing of their loved ones, as it is such an emotional experience to have someone come in with a heavy heart, and have the weight of grief taken off of their shoulders. Every person who comes to us is special and it is wonderful to hear all their stories and experiences.

People often ask me if I too am a medium and, although my talents do lean toward the psychic side and I am very "sensitive" to people's energy, I do not have Patrick's amazing abilities. I witnessed him develop his natural gift and I encouraged him every step of the way. When Patrick is giving a reading, I can "feel" what the person receiving the reading is feeling, as well as pick up on the spirit's emotions. At times, I do even hear a word or two from spirits.

———

Working alongside my brother Patrick, I have been privy to many different scenarios and stories of people's lives. I can tell you that through these readings, I have heard of some glorious lives that have played out in extraordinary ways, as well as some tragic and heartbreaking lives that have made me weep. I have heard of great love stories that even an epic movie could not match and I have heard of desperately lonely people who felt that they were very much alone in this world.

The one common denominator of them all is that no matter what the circumstance, it was love that carried them through and it is love that keeps them going.

I began this book by explaining what love is and why it is so important to give and receive it. Although I will delve into love and how it is so critical to all aspects of life, I will then return to romantic love as that is the main focus of this book.

Patrick shares readings in Part Two as well as throughout this book that illustrate how love can bring joy, happiness, sadness, and yes, hardship, to any relationship. The examples and lessons learned from these readings will let you in on great wisdom about life and love from those in spirit.

Part Three will lend you a hand in moving forward in your life, along with your loved ones in spirit, and give you a new perspective on how their love and continuing guidance will help you through every day of your life.

Part Four will illustrate the connections you already have with your loved ones in spirit and explain how to maintain your connections or restart them with those you love.

In Part Five, I want to give you some tools in the form of romantic meditations that will take you and your love on several amazing journeys. Some of the most beautiful envisioned locations can be yours instantly and can take you and your love on a trip that will not only relax you, but help you understand each other better. These meditations can involve our loved ones who have passed or that special someone you may have in mind who is in your life now. Each time you take these detailed journeys, you'll be able to relax, enjoy the new surroundings, love each other more, and your relationship will grow even stronger.

On a previous page, you read how a dictionary defines the word, love. As you can see, it is hard to put into words just what love is, as love itself can be simplistic and yet at the same time complicated. True love is real; it is concrete and becomes a part of our souls. Think about it—love can change the way we feel, it can make us well if we are sick, it changes our personality by making us giddy, nervous, unsure, and yet the happiest we have ever been. It is the element of life most of us strive for and try to nourish once it is achieved.

Why?

Because love feeds the soul!

There are a few things in this life of which I am certain:

- Life … is continuous.
- Death … does not exist.
- Love … is life.

PART ONE

UNDERSTANDING LOVE

I want to start this book by explaining my views on Love and how important it is in living this life. The more the mystery of that thing called Love is understood, the more prevalent it will become in life. Love is the foundation of our souls and branches out to compassion, caring, nurturing, and giving hope to others.

In the following pages, I want to illustrate the importance of love and why you need to have it, and also give it, in your life.

1. Love Never Dies

———

Life does not exist without love. When we are born, we cannot survive without the love of someone to feed us and help us grow; and in turn, we love those who have shown us this dedication and care. Then our bodies grow to young adulthood and we start to look for love in a partner, someone with whom we can start a life of our own and perhaps have a family together. Then we grow older, and we need the love of our families when we no longer are able to care for ourselves.

All that love, a lifetime of it, forms us to become who we are, our souls, and that is what we will take to Heaven with us when we pass over to the other side.

I like to look at love as a diamond. It is beautiful, has many facets, many sides to it, and it is one of the most precious objects on earth. We would all like to have one, yet it can be arduous to acquire. But the real beauty of a diamond is in its rarity and its fire. What do I mean by fire? A gem is not only measured in carats but in its fire or brilliance. If you look at each facet of a precious stone, you will see many colors, such as those found in a diamond, which may seem to be clear or colorless from afar.

That is a good analogy for love.

It can seem like a simple, singular emotion, but it is much more complicated than that. Love stems from the heart of our soul and it branches out like a tree, as there are many types of love. There is the wonderful unconditional love between a parent and a child, there is the love for other family members, the romantic love between two people, the love between friends, and of course, even the love we have for our pets. And all of this love that is shared and received connects us to each other.

But alas, I must keep to the theme to which this book is dedicated, and that is romantic love, the falling in love kind of love, true love. You know, the Romeo and Juliet, Scarlett O'Hara and Rhett Butler, Edward and Bella kind of love. And who doesn't like hearing the story of love that is written in the stars, so strong yet so difficult to obtain.

The story of two people coming together starts out many times as simple attraction. It can be a physical attraction, personality attraction, emotional attraction, or a combination of all these—a spark, if you will, that ignites the embers of romance to keep the fires of love burning forever! (Hey, what do you expect? My father was a songwriter and I inherited his love of words.)

Romantic love can take over the mind, the body, and the soul. It can make you seem crazy for the other person to the point that nothing else in the world matters. Ah, if only everyone could experience this kind of love and it would last forever—that would be wonderful. But in the real world, love can and most likely will change.

And believe it or not, that is good.

The love you have for one another is a living entity and it changes as you change. Ask any couple who has been in a long-term relationship. The person you are with at the beginning of a relationship is not going to be the person you are with in the future, nor are you going to be the same as you were in the past. As a person grows, they change physically, mentally, and emotionally, and the one who loves them must be committed and accept these changes, growing along with that person.

That is what long-lasting love is all about.

Many potential obstacles will come along that a couple in love may not consider at the beginning of their liaison. Jobs, home, bills, children, and so on. All of this "life" stuff happens to everyone, and it can sometimes push down or suppress the feeling of love.

All of this is how our souls grow, as does our love, by experiencing such challenges. But with a strong sense of dedication between any two people, there will be soul growth and true love can come out on top!

Love in Spirit

Along with the joy one can experience with love, the opposite can also appear. That is the heartache one can experience when a person you love passes into spirit.

When someone you were in love with dies, you may
feel as if a part of you has also died. You may have the
feelings of loss, anger, sadness, and loneliness that can con-
sume you, bring you to your knees, emotionally as well as
physically, depending on how deep the love was.

And why?

In this physical world, people are accustomed to experiencing life with the typical five senses. And when a loved
one passes into spirit, the person still here can feel as if they
no longer are able to hear, feel, or even see them. Therefore,
that person might feel as if the one they loved no longer
exists and their relationship has ended.

This is where people can often be surprised!

————

When a person passes, they become spirit, meaning their
soul disconnects from their body. But don't be mistaken;
just because the soul leaves the body, it does not mean the
soul of a loved one will leave you. It is quite the opposite.

When a person passes into spirit, they are still that person. Yes, they now live by a different set of physics, which
we are unable to comprehend, but they continue on, having

the same physical attributes as they had here, such as a body, including their five senses. But when they transcend into spirit, they will also acquire other senses and abilities that we are unable to comprehend in this physical world. But remember, your loved one in spirit can still see you, hear and feel you, as well as being able to understand your thoughts. Being in spirit, they also have the advantage of seeing the path you are on and in which direction you are headed. By having this ability, they can guide you by giving you thoughts, feelings, and signs, all of which can help you on your life's journey. And as is true with all that is in Heaven, and since all things are possible, that which brings a spirit the most happiness is their ability to love you and to receive your love back.

This is why it is important that when someone you love passes into spirit, you perceive them as being the same person they were (of course, they are now smarter about all of this "life" stuff). And know that they are and will always continue to be a part of your life.

A person in spirit carries the same emotions they had when they were in the physical realm, but emotion becomes stronger as the physical mind no longer filters or eliminates it. In this present body, we usually think with our minds, but when it comes to love, that emotion usually takes over our minds. How many times have you heard the expression that "love is blind" or "don't think with your heart"? This happens when emotions take over and our minds take a back seat to their effects. In spirit, emotions are always front and center and are what guide a spirit. And the strongest feeling a spirit has is love, as it is truly the essence of who we are as humans.

This is why it is critical to understand that not only do your loved ones never die, but neither does their love for you.

Benefits of Maintaining a Love Connection

Many people think of Heaven as a place where we go when we die and we live a separate life, to be joined one day by those we loved here on this Earth. This is a misconception of what Heaven really is.

Although no one is an expert on what Heaven and God truly are, I can tell you, judging by the many lessons that I have learned through the readings Patrick has given, that there are some truths we can comprehend.

Life continues after this one and the ties with our loved ones become stronger in spirit. There is no separation between your loved ones in spirit and yourself and the bond you once shared not only continues but grows.

In this life, everything you do and know is based on what you perceive, and how you perceive things is how you come to an understanding. How you understand things will determine how you move forward in your life.

A person who does not believe in the afterlife will usually experience more grief when a loved one passes into spirit than a person who does believe. This is because a nonbeliever thinks their loved one who has passed just dies and they no longer exist, and that the only parts of them left are the memories of what once was.

This belief will lead a person to disconnect with a loved one in spirit, a connection that does still exist. Of course, a spirit will still connect with their loved one even if that person doesn't believe in God, an afterlife or that their loved ones are still with them. A person in spirit will always continue to love and guide their loved one, even if there is no acknowledgment of their existence. However, the nonbeliever will continue on without all the benefits that come with knowing their loved one remains a part of their life.

For those who do believe in an afterlife, although there is still heartache, there is also hope. Hope that a loved one is still with them and hope that they will be reunited with them one day. This hope can eventually ease the pain of a person's passing and aid in the life the one on Earth still enjoys.

But the one driving goal that Patrick and I both hold is to help people go one step further, to not only hope or believe there is an afterlife, but to KNOW there is one.

And once a person knows this, their relationship with a loved one in spirit grows even stronger.

————

So in the following pages, our hope is that you will experience and learn from the stories we share of readings Patrick has given that were inspired by love. As you read on, you may even find yourself relating to many of these life experiences and perhaps come to a greater understanding of what this life, your life, is all about:

Love.

PART TWO

❧

LOVE
STORIES

When I am about to give a reading to someone, for me it is as if I am about to open a new book to read, as I am to be taken on a journey through someone's life.

And as Kathy and I always say, "EVERYONE has a story."

In the following part, I will share with you what I have found to be memorable and instructive readings I have given, each with some life lessons from which all can learn and benefit.

2. Pages of Life and Love

When you are reading a book, you find that a story starts to unfold with each page turned, taking you on a special trip the author wants you to experience. This is what I experience each time I make a connection with someone's loved one in spirit. I am not the author of their story, only a participant, and when I am giving a reading, I never know what is going to be said or where the reading is going to go, all I know is that I am there along for the ride.

When giving readings, a person's story, along with their spirit loved one's story, will come alive as their experiences, feelings, and insights on their relationship are revealed during the process. I always find it amazing how caught up I, too, become in their lives and relationships as the connections are made, not only by experiencing what is being said at the reading, but even more so by the powerful feelings and emotions that I am experiencing from both my client and their loved one in spirit.

For the most part, the people who come to me will want me to make a connection with those in spirit with whom they were closest in life, usually someone they did and still do love very much. And since I am able to feel all the love that a spirit has to give, a love that is in its purest form, this is something that I will never be able to describe. The closest description I can give in words is that it is truly the essence of life.

————

With the many readings I have given throughout the years, the ones that I enjoy the most are the ones that help people to make the love bonds with their loved ones in spirit even stronger.

Whether it is confirming the love they have already been receiving and feeling from a spirit, or helping them to understand how to open up and receive the love that their loved ones in spirit have to give, or even having a loved one in spirit help guide them into the future with the possibility of finding more love in their lives, these are the some of the most powerful readings I can give.

The one truth I know is that there is no right or wrong way for you to have love in this life—as it is up to each individual how they want to experience it. Whether it is to fall in love with a lover and spend a short time or a lifetime with them, or if it is to love family and friends who are in your life (that of course includes your pets as your family members), this is what the essence of life is really all about.

I have spoken with some of the most successful people on this earth, from the richest to the most famous. Even with all their success and money, some of them feel they are still living a sad and unfulfilled life by not having someone with whom they can share their life.

Life is about love; and without receiving it or giving it, you really are not living.

3. Hand in Hand

There is one phone call that you never expect to receive and if it happens, it changes your life forever...

Rebecca and Todd kissed their two children goodnight as they tucked their twins into bed. It was a cold snowy January night and the whole family was exhausted after a day of playing in the snow. After the young boys fell asleep, Todd, working the late shift that night, had to leave for his job. Rebecca hugged her husband and told him to be safe. His departing words to her were, "Always, honey," as he smiled and closed the door behind him.

That night, for some reason, Rebecca was having trouble falling asleep. She tossed and turned for what seemed to be hours and finally, as her body started to drift into sleep, the phone rang. Rebecca, still groggy, picked up the phone to answer it, and within a matter of minutes, the message she heard on the other end had her fully awake.

Rebecca was told that her husband Todd had been in a car accident and she needed to come to the hospital right away.

In a panic and yet still calm, Rebecca called neighbors to inform them of what had happened and asked them to watch her children.

Once Rebecca arrived at the hospital, she was hurriedly escorted to the ICU. There, Todd, the man she loved, the father to their children, the man that just a few hours before was having snowball fights with his family... lay there, helpless and motionless. The doctor and a police officer approached Rebecca and told her what they thought had happened. Apparently Todd's car had hit a patch of black ice, which made him lose control of his car and it plunged off an embankment, hitting some trees. They explained that his injuries were severe and that he was not likely to regain consciousness, and would not survive the night.

Hearing this news, Rebecca could feel her legs start to give out from underneath her as the police officer caught her and lowered her into a chair. After a few deep breaths, Rebecca regained her composure and asked the doctor if there was anything more he could do, but there was not.

Rebecca stood up and went to the side of Todd's bed, grabbing the railing as it took everything she had for her trembling legs not to give out again. She told herself she had to be strong now for Todd.

As she stood by his side, she took his powerful large hand and placed it in hers. She gazed at his peaceful face and, with tears streaming down her cheeks, found it difficult not to believe that Todd was just sleeping and would soon wake up and go home with her. But she knew deep inside that this was not to be.

"Todd, Todd, can you hear me, honey?" she asked, but received no answer. The doctor approached Rebecca and explained that due to the head injuries, it was unlikely that Todd could hear her. But Rebecca continued squeezing Todd's hand and speaking with her husband, telling him how much she loved him and how the children needed him to get better.

As Rebecca continued talking with Todd, suddenly she felt his hand start squeezing hers back. She gasped and shouted out, "Todd, Todd, can you hear me?" Todd squeezed her hand even harder and began making a loud, grunting noise. A minute or two later, Todd opened his eyes to just a slit. Rebecca could see Todd's beautiful green eyes, and it seemed to take all the energy he had to give her a weak smile.

Holding hands and with tears starting to form in Todd's eyes, he muttered two words to his loving wife Rebecca, "Love you." These were Todd's last words as with that, the hand that Rebecca was holding, the hand that she held on their first date, the hand she had held as they walked down the aisle, began to release itself from hers as Todd took his last breath and closed his eyes.

Rebecca became hysterical and began crying out to Todd, "Don't go, Todd. Don't go..."

It was about a year after the accident when I spoke with Rebecca. She had read my books and hoped that I would be able to speak with Todd. Rebecca got her wish.

"Your husband has a strong emotional spirit," I said to Rebecca. "I can tell by the way he is connecting with me that he is not too shy to show his feelings!"

Rebecca anxiously replied, "That sounds like Todd! Todd always wore his heart on his sleeve."

"I can tell by his personality that when he was happy, you knew it, and when he was angry, you knew that, too."

"Very true," Rebecca replied.

I continued. "Well, let me tell you, he is also good at giving love as not only is he saying it to you, but I can feel his love strongly for you."

Rebecca started to cry at hearing this message.

"Todd is telling me that his passing was quick and easy and there was no pain at all for him."

"Oh God, I was hoping to hear that," Rebecca replied.

"It is true. Was he in some type of accident?" I asked. "He is showing me a car."

"Yes, that's exactly what happened. He was in a car accident that took his life," Rebecca affirmed.

I told Rebecca, "Todd again wants to assure you that he felt absolutely no pain."

Rebecca seemed to take comfort at hearing this from Todd.

I continued. "Todd also wants you to know not only was it an accident, it was his time to be in spirit. He keeps repeating, it was his time, it was his time."

"I know it was an accident, but I don't understand it being his time. He was so young and he had children that needed him. How could it have been his time?"

I replied, "Todd understands exactly what you are saying but wants you to know that in spirit, all is understood, and you learn all the answers to the whys in this life. He says that he now knows a lot more than you about what life means and how it works, and wants you to trust him when he tells you that there is a reason for everything, even his passing."

Rebecca answered, "I can only hold faith in that being true."

"Todd says you have always had faith in him and knows that you always will."

"Yes, I will," Rebecca replied.

I continued. "He is talking about children and is showing me two fingers, do you have two children?"

"Yes!" Rebecca shouted. "Two sons."

At that moment, I felt another extreme emanation of love from Todd for his children.

"Todd loves his boys so very much. He is telling me that you have been doing a fantastic job in raising your boys."

"I was hoping he was able to look down from Heaven and check on us every now and then."

"Check on you every now and then? Todd wants me to tell you that he is not only with you and your sons every single day, he is helping you in ways you could never imagine."

"How is that possible?"

"Keep in mind that he is still very much the same person he once was—the man you married and the father of your children. And even though you may not see him, he is a big part of your family and your lives. There was nothing more important in this physical life than you and his children and that hasn't changed, even in spirit. He also wants you to know that he is able to help guide you down certain paths that you and your boys will take in the future."

Rebecca asked, "He can?"

I answered, "Yes, he can! But he is telling me that he does wish you would listen to him more often, but that was always the case between you two."

Rebecca laughed out loud at what her husband was telling her.

"Todd is now sounding like a proud dad and is telling me something about your boys starting school," I said.

"Yes, we have twin boys, and they started their first day of school just a few weeks ago. I kept thinking how Todd would have loved to have been a part of this."

"He did see it! And not only that, he's bragging that he was able to be with them the entire day!"

"Really? I felt so sad leaving them that first day, I wanted more than anything to be there with them."

"Todd wants you to know that they both did just fine."

Rebecca replied, "That is what the teacher said to me as well."

"Todd wants you to know that one of the greatest benefits of being in spirit is that there is never going to be a moment in you and your boys' lives that he too won't be able to experience."

Rebecca started to tear up again at hearing this from Todd.

I continued. "Todd is behind you right now and is stroking your hair. He wants you to know that he made you a promise to take care of you and that he is doing this in more ways than you could ever imagine."

Rebecca continued to cry as I continued speaking.

"Todd is saying something about how you are listening to music in his honor, but he is laughing because you hate that style of music. Is this true?"

This brought a smile to Rebecca's face.

She said, "Yes, I have been listening to country music. That was something Todd loved and I did not. When we would drive somewhere, he would always crank it up in the car and sing out loud with it; even if he didn't know the words, he would just make them up. I still really can't stand hearing it, but I sometimes will tune it in on the radio just to remember those times with him."

"He wants you to know that he's still in the car with you and that puts a smile on his face. He is telling me that you make him laugh because he's caught you singing along with some of the songs!" I said.

"I do not sing those songs!" Rebecca shouted, with a smile on her face as if she'd just been caught.

"Todd is saying you do, and I know that spirits don't lie," I said, with a grin.

"Okay, okay, maybe a word or two, but I guess I don't realize that I'm doing it."

Todd says, "Sure you don't…"

Todd wanted to talk about something else and by the change in his energy, I recognized that it was a serious message he wanted to get through. I listened intently to what Todd had to say.

"Todd now wants to talk about something that he knows you don't want to hear, but he says it is important for you to listen."

"What is it?" Rebecca asked.

Once I received the message from Todd, I took a moment to ask him if he was sure he wanted to bring this up now. I already knew of course that he was aware of what he was doing, but I also knew that I was the one who was going to receive the response to what he was asking, and I am never sure how someone is going to respond to a life-changing request from a spirit.

I took a deep breath and repeated what Todd had said to me…

"Todd is telling me that he wants you to be open to finding another love."

With that, an expression of shock came across Rebecca's face as tears started to stream down her face.

"Why!? Why would he say that to me?" Rebecca asked.

I waited a moment to receive Todd's response.

"He is telling me that you are the type of person who needs to express love. You have loved him and always will, and of course he knows this, just as he loves you. But as you continue your life, your continuing to give love is not only important to you, but it is also important to those who will receive it. He wants you to know that it would be very selfish of him to deny another person your gift, which is the unlimited amount of love you have to offer. He wants you to know that it made him the man he was and is, and that your love will always be a part of him. He wants you to know that if you were to fall in love with another person, he knows that this would never take away the love you have for him. The love you two share is eternal, and Todd says that his utmost desire in Heaven is for you to be happy. Always remember that your happiness is his happiness."

Rebecca thought about what she was hearing, and as she wiped away more tears, she responded, "I just don't know if I could ever open myself up to having another relationship. I love Todd so much and even though it has been over a year since his passing, I would feel as if I were cheating on him."

I told her, "Todd is smiling and states that you are at your happiest when you are taking care of and loving people. This is why it is so important that you continue to do so, this is who you are!"

"That is easier said than done," Rebecca replied. "And I just don't want Todd to think I don't love him anymore."

"You now know that is not the case. He wants nothing more in both of your lives than for you to be happy."

"What would happen if I do find someone new? Would Todd leave me?" Rebecca asked.

I felt Todd's strong personality as he flooded my senses with his love for her as well as his determination to watch over her.

"Of course not. He wants you to know that he will never leave you. He is telling me it is not like he would say, 'Okay, she's got a new love, time for me to hit the road!' Yes, you may have another husband here, but guess what? You'll still have a his love in spirit! He wants you to know that when in spirit, you become a little smarter on all this 'life' stuff and promises you that he won't be jealous. If you do find another love, he knows that you will still love him as much as you ever did before. Your love for each other is eternal."

A look of relief appeared on Rebecca's face.

I could also tell by feeling Todd's emotions that he wanted to lighten up the mood of the conversation.

I continued. "Todd also wants me to tell you that if you find another relationship, you never have to worry about being intimate with him, if you know what he means… Todd will know when the 'Do Not Disturb' sign is on the door!" I relayed the message with a smile.

"I was wondering how that would work!" Rebecca chuckled.

I told Rebecca, "Todd says don't ever worry about that, and don't forget, there are things for him to do in Heaven as well…"

"Hey, what does that mean?" Rebecca said with a laugh.

"Oh, that when you're having fun, let's just say that he's having fun too!"

"Now I'm starting to get jealous!" Rebecca shouted at Todd.

"He is telling me you don't have to be. He wants you to know that even being with all of the angels in Heaven, you're the prettiest angel of all."

Rebecca smiled through tears of happiness and said, "Now that truly is Todd…"

———

Rebecca understood everything Todd had relayed to her in the reading. She told me that even though she did not know what her next steps would be, she now understood that Todd was always going to be with her and the children. With that reassurance, she might consider being open to finding happiness once again.

Rebecca checked back with me about a year later and told me that she had started having feelings for a new guy she had been seeing and it was now developing into a serious relationship. She never thought this would happen, but because of what Todd had said to her, she had placed herself in the mindset that it was all right for her to find happiness again, without guilt.

Rebecca said that, interestingly, she felt that Todd had something to do with her meeting this new man. And why? Because both this new guy and Todd had something in common…

Their love for country music.

Rebecca knew Todd had his hand in this, and it brought a smile to her face.

4. Being Content

―――――

A woman named Madeline, or Maddie, as she likes to be called, made a phone appointment for me to connect with the love of her life, her husband Bruce.

Bruce and Maddie grew up in the same neighborhood. Bruce was a couple of years older than Maddie and was friends with her older brother, Ben. Maddie came from a family of six siblings and was the baby of the family. Boys being boys, Bruce never paid much attention to Maddie when he and Ben hung out, but when he did see her from time to time at the house, he would always say "hi" to her. As the years went by, Maddie saw less and less of Bruce as he and Ben started to go their separate ways.

One early morning when she was attending high school, while waiting for her friend to pick her up for school, Maddie saw a younger boy being bullied while waiting for his bus to arrive. She saw that two older boys were picking on him *because he was wearing hand-me-down clothes that were dingy and torn. Not able to stand it any longer, she started to go toward the boys when, out of nowhere, another older guy appeared and approached the younger boys. It was Bruce, someone she hadn't seen in a few years. The first thing she noticed about Bruce was that he had filled out nicely since she had last seen him and was quite intimidating toward the other two boys. Bruce grabbed one bully by the scruff of the neck and asked if there was a problem. The bullies shook their heads no and he let the boy down. He then told the two boys that the kid they were picking on was his cousin and if they ever messed with him again, they were going to have to deal with him. The boys nodded and told Bruce there was nothing to worry about and shook the little boy's hand. Bruce told his pretend cousin to let him know if either of them gave him trouble again, and turned to leave, when he spotted Maddie standing nearby, watching what had taken place. She thought what she had just witnessed Bruce doing was wonderful. She had never realized how big and strong he had become, and Bruce was surprised to see that Ben's little sister had grown up and was now a beautiful young girl. The two couldn't take their eyes off each other from that moment on, and they never did. They dated all through school and married soon after graduation.*

Bruce was a carpenter by trade and enjoyed making furniture in his spare time when he was not out doing repair work for people around town. Maddie was a stay-at-home mother, content taking care of their two children. Bruce was known around town for his talent of working with his hands, and even though he would charge people for the work he did, he would often offer his services free of charge if he knew it would help a person in need. This was something his father had done and he was proud to do the same. Bruce also had a great sense of humor and loved to make people laugh. There was nothing more important to Bruce than putting a smile on Maddie's face. And though it seemed that Maddie and Bruce never had a lot to their name, what they lacked in possessions, their love for each other and their family made up for in tenfold measure.

As the years went by, Bruce and Maddie raised two wonderful children, a son and a daughter, and when the last one left the house, they both smiled though tears, knowing that they at least still had each other.

Unfortunately, it was not going to be for long.

A few months after their daughter left the house and the two were adjusting to their empty nest, while working in his shop, Bruce didn't feel right. He thought it was just a stomach bug and decided to keep it to himself and not tell Maddie, as he did not want her to worry. But that secret did not last long, as Maddie could sense that something was wrong with her husband. When Maddie asked Bruce how he was feeling, he told her he just had the stomach flu and assured her he'd be better in a day or two. That day or two turned into weeks and Bruce's illness started to become worse. Maddie kept suggesting that Bruce go to the doctor, but she knew that her words went in one ear and out the other, as Bruce did not believe much in *what doctors could do. He had always joked in the past that he was in perfect health because he never went to them.*

One afternoon, Bruce decided to get some air and pay a visit to his workshop, to finish sanding a table he had been working on. Bruce thought getting outdoors and into the fresh air would do him good and take his mind off the pain that kept getting stronger in his stomach. Maddie knew Bruce was weak and decided to keep a close eye on him, as she was nervous about him handling dangerous tools in his condition.

As Bruce slowly started gathering his tools, suddenly he bent over and collapsed on the floor. Maddie rushed to his side and immediately called 911. Bruce was taken to the hospital and after a battery of tests, the couple was given the devastating news that Bruce had developed advanced stomach cancer. Of course Bruce being Bruce, he took the news by making a joke and asking the doctor if he was sure it wasn't caused by his wife's cooking. Through tears, Maddie slapped Bruce's arm and told him to behave himself. But that was Bruce, always making a joke.

Bruce passed away several weeks later surrounded by his loved ones. As Maddie held his hand, Bruce's last words to Maddie were to tell her how much he loved her and that he would always be watching over her and their family. He also told her that he would be sure to put in a good word for her with God…

———

Several years after Bruce's passing, Maddie was able to make a phone appointment with me. When Maddie called me for her appointment, I could tell how excited she was to hear from her husband. I gave her a brief overview about how I work and she understood what was about to take place. As in all of my readings, I took a deep breath and opened myself up for spirit communication. It took no time at all for her husband to make his connection with me.

"Maddie, I can already tell you that your husband is here," I said.

"Already?" Maddie replied.

"Yes. I can sense that he is a very strong spirit and that too is also how he was in this physical world."

"Oh yes. Bruce is a very strong person," she replied.

"I can also tell that he has a great sense of humor because he wants you to know that he likes the fact that he can spy on you now without you knowing it, just like you would do with him. But it's a lot easier when you're invisible like he is."

This made Maddie laugh. "I never spied on him!"

"Maddie, Bruce is telling me different!" I responded. "And spirits always tell me the truth!"

"Okay, okay, maybe just a little," she admitted.

Bruce and I started to laugh. "Well, he says that it was just to make sure he wasn't getting into trouble."

"I agree with that!" Maddie replied. "But he never did."

As I continued, I asked Bruce to indicate how he passed over into spirit.

"Bruce is making my stomach hurt; did he pass with some type of a stomach or intestinal problem?"

"He did. Bruce had stomach cancer," Maddie replied, with sadness in her voice.

"He wants you to know that he is in perfect health now!" I said.

"I know he is," Maddie said.

If the discussion of a passing comes up during a reading, this can be a sensitive and emotional subject. But what Bruce said next started to make me laugh and I hoped that it would be the same for Maddie.

I told Maddie, "Bruce is telling me as he is laughing that it wasn't the cancer that killed him, but your cooking!"

I waited to hear the response Maddie would give to Bruce's statement. Thank goodness, she again laughed.

"It was not!" Maddie said, laughing hard now. "Bruce always joked about my cooking, but he sure polished off every bite on his plate!"

"I am sure he is just saying this as a confirmation for you," I said. "Though a strange and funny confirmation it is!"

"That's Bruce!" Maddie replied happily.

"Bruce is also conveying to me that he did not like doctors."

"Not at all, he never went to them," Maddie affirmed.

"He is saying why should he have; he had never been sick a day in his life."

"That is true."

I continued. "He's saying that even if he had listened to you and had seen the doctor earlier, it would not have made a difference. It was his time to pass."

I could hear sniffling over the phone coming from Maddie.

I continued. "Bruce is telling me that you know he is right. He also wants you to know what helped to make the pain go away was having you and his family by his side."

"Oh, I am so happy to hear that! Yes, our children and I were by his bedside," Maddie confirmed.

The reading continued and after some messages to his children, the subject changed to Maddie and Bruce's relationship.

"Bruce is telling me that you and he are soul mates."

Maddie responded defiantly, "Yes, we are!"

"He wants you to know how true that is and that his love for you is forever."

Maddie said with much love in her voice, "And mine for him."

"Bruce is telling me that you speak to him all the time and he wants you to know that he hears every word. Not from Heaven, but by your side," I told her.

"I can feel him with me," Maddie said softly.

"Funny thing is, Bruce knows you can and it makes him just as happy as it does you!"

"I always ask Bruce what I should do about any given subject, and I do listen back to his answer."

"He is saying to me that it is about time you listened to him," I said with the chuckle that Bruce was relaying with his answer.

"That's not true; he knows I always listened to him."

"Bruce is telling me that you are living your life as if the only thing that has changed is that he is invisible now."

Many times during a reading, a loved one in spirit will bring up insights on what the future holds for the person to whom I am giving the reading, even if it's speaking about a possible new relationship in this life. And this is what Bruce wanted to speak about next.

"Bruce is telling me that you are still a young woman and that men are still falling at your feet."

"Tell him to behave himself," she retorted, seeming a little embarrassed.

"He says it is true! He also is stating that you still have such a long life ahead, you certainly have his permission, not that you need it, to be open to finding a new love. But I have to tell you that the way Bruce is telling me this, almost laughing, this is something that you are not even considering."

Maddie responded, "He knows me all too well! Bruce was my husband, still is my husband and will always be my husband. I have no interest in finding another love, as I already have one! Bruce was and is my one and only, and this is what carries me through day to day. We will be together in spirit one day, and don't get me wrong; I am not wishing that day to come soon. But I have too much still to do here. I know there is a reason for him to be in spirit and my time will come one day. Until that day, he will be with me, loving me, and I am content with this."

I could feel Bruce was very proud of his love and I responded, "This could not make Bruce any happier."

"So tell Bruce that he better not be looking at any other girls up there!" Maddie said.

I laughed, as did Bruce, and I responded, "He wants you to know that you never have to worry about that, as you still have his heart, even in Heaven…

With that, Maddie teared up, but with tears of happiness.

———————

After the reading, Maddie told me that even though she missed Bruce being in this physical dimension, she was happy living her life, knowing that Bruce was still with her. Maddie said that not a day went by that she did not talk with her husband, asking for his advice or opinion about something, and even though she may not always hear an answer from him, she knew that he was there, taking care of her as he always had.

Depending on where a person is in their life's journey, their circumstance and state of mind will determine what a spirit can convey to their loved one as far as how to move forward. In this case, Bruce did not express any concerns or disagreements on how Maddie was continuing to live her life.

Many times, it is important for a person to go on with their life and be open to the possibility of finding a new love, as it is a gift to be shared. But there can be cases like Maddie's, where she was perfectly content with her life and the love she had with her husband Bruce. Maddie felt that Bruce was the only man she would or could ever love. Bruce understood this and had the same sentiments. This was a union that had endured the test of time and would continue to do so in the hereafter.

5. HIDDEN LOVE

———

Roommates Alan and Chris had just completed their workout at the gym after spending an hour or so taking turns encouraging one another as they went through their training circuit. Both men were in their mid-twenties and their physique showed that they were dedicated to living a healthy and fit lifestyle. After leaving the gym, the two drove to one of their favorite hangouts to meet up with Alan's brother, William, and his wife, Sharon, for a relaxing dinner. While eating and catching up on what they had all been doing, the conversation turned to when Alan was going to finally settle down and find Miss Right. This was not a new conversation, as William, being the older brother, liked to tease Alan about his romantic life. Alan just grinned and said to William that you never know when the right one is right in front of you. William laughed, agreeing with Alan, as he glanced around, checking out all the females who were in the bar area of the restaurant.

Once dinner had concluded, Alan and Chris said good-night to William and Sharon, and the two men went back to their car. Inside, the two looked at each other and started laughing. Chris asked Alan, "Do you think they know?" Alan replied "No way!"

The two men smiled, leaned in to one another and kissed.

Alan and Chris had met in the gym a year before and struck up a conversation. The two found that they had many common interests such as their study of nutrition, a passion for entertainment, and a love of sports, especially their football team, the Miami Dolphins. After a few weeks of meeting at the gym and hanging out with each other, they also found out they had something else in common: Both men were gay.

It didn't take long for Alan and Chris to develop romantic feelings for one another and after several months, the two decided to move in together. Living in Los Angeles, California, with such a high cost of living, it is not uncommon for people to live together, so Alan and Chris were certain that no one would think twice about the two living together and the nature of their true relationship.

As time went on, both men were falling more and more in love with each other and found that living together brought both of them such happiness that neither of them had ever experienced before. They would often go hiking in the mountains, or just stay in bed on rainy days. Chris loved the way Alan would make him laugh and how they would tease one another. Neither one had ever experienced such love before and believed their relationship would stand the test of time.

Chris had already been out about his sexuality with his family and friends, but Alan had not yet been so open with his. Not that Alan was in any way ashamed of being gay; he just never felt the time was right to tell his family. Alan knew that if he came out, his parents would wonder what it was that they did wrong, and he didn't want to deal with what they would say to him and all the questions that were to follow. Alan's father was an ex-Marine and a man's man. While Alan was growing up, it was not uncommon for his father to use gay slurs every now and then. His father, like many others, had the idea that being gay meant that even though you were a male, you must also be feminine and less of a man. Alan also thought the same. That is, until he started to have feelings for the same sex himself.

As a teenager, Alan first started to feel sexually attracted to men. These feelings were something he would often push away as he was confused by having an attraction to guys while yet not fitting into the "gay stereotypical mold" his father would often ridicule. Here he was, captain of his football team, he also played baseball, and was even known to be the ladies' man around school. He would often date girls, trying to convince himself that his attraction to guys was just a phase, something he would eventually grow out of if he just lived a "straight" man's life.

But as time went on, and no matter how long or how hard Alan tried, his attraction to men remained. After graduating from high school and entering college, Alan found himself in a situation that made it clear to him that his attraction to men *was not just a phase. One evening, Alan was at a party where everyone was having a good time drinking and acting a little crazy. At one point, Alan was challenged to play "gay chicken"; this is where two guys stand in front of one another and are dared to kiss each other on the lips. Alan said he was up to the dare and then was able to point out the person he wanted to kiss. Alan knew many of the people at the party but pointed to a young man he did not know, but to whom he felt attracted. The man, not wanting to look like a wimp, decided to accept the dare after the crowd started to heckle him. So the two men stood face to face, and after a few false attempts, their lips finally connected and the two kissed each other as the crowd yelled wildly. After the kiss, the two pulled back, wiped their mouths and pretended to spit out the spittle. Everyone in the room laughed, but it was much more than a joke and a dare for Alan. Alan actually enjoyed kissing this guy, something he had fantasized about in the past but never had the courage to do. Alan knew that this night was a turning point in his life and finally decided that it was time to give in to his true feelings. As time went on and his exploration with men continued, Alan finally accepted his sexuality, that of being a gay man.*

But just as in the past when he dated women, Alan decided to continue to keep his love life private from his family.

———

On their way home from that dinner with Alan's brother and sister-in-law, the two men resumed the discussion they had had so often about when Alan was going to finally come out to his family. Alan was becoming more and more comfortable with the idea and wanted to show his family, especially his father, that being gay was a sexual orientation, not a personality flaw.

After stopping at a red light, once the traffic light turned green, as the cars in his lane started to move, Chris turned to Alan and yelled out "WATCH IT!" But it was too late. Another car ran right into the driver's side of their vehicle.

When Chris woke up in the hospital the next day he was told that he and Alan and been hit by a drunk driver. All he wanted to know was Alan's condition. Chris was told that although his injuries were serious, he would recover completely. Chris was then told the sad news—that Alan did not survive the crash.

———

When Chris came to see me just a few months after the accident, he was receptive to a reading, yet nervous at the same time. I told him that it was natural to be a little anxious if he had never spoken with a medium before and that he should just relax. I asked Chris about the relationship of the person he would like for me to make a connection with, and he told me it was a male friend.

As I opened myself up, I could feel the presence of a male friend immediately.

"Your friend is here," I said to Chris. "But I have to say this right off the top. One of the things I am blessed with is being able to feel the love a spirit has for someone I am reading to, and I can tell by the love this guy has for you that you two were more than just friends, correct?"

Chris started to tear up and quietly replied, "Yes."

"Now don't try to fool me," I said with a smile. "I can always tell what a spirit's feeling is for a person and I know the difference between the love of a friend and a lover."

"Sorry, I just didn't know what Alan wanted to bring up."

"Well, Alan wants you to know how much he loved you and still does!" I told him.

"I love him so very much too," Chris said, clenching his fists with anxiety.

"Alan is telling me about his passing and I am feeling from him that it was an unnatural passing, was this from an accident?"

"Yes," Chris replied.

"But I will also tell you that it was very quick for him and he did not feel any pain."

"I was hoping for that," he said, with a look of relief on his face.

"He is mentioning something about not being alone in the car; you were with him, I believe."

Chris started to cry. "I was. Alan was driving and we were sideswiped by a drunk driver."

I reassured Chris he had nothing to fear, and continued. "Alan wants you to know that he is okay and that he also knows how sorry the driver of the other car feels about the accident. He wants you to know that he forgives him and wants you to do the same."

"Alan must know that's not going to happen any time soon," Chris spat out in an angry response.

"He knows that it will take time, but you need to let it go. He says if he can, you can. He says he's the one who got killed anyway!" I relayed to Chris.

Even though I could tell that Alan was saying that with a smile, I was not sure how Chris was going to react to what Alan had said. I don't censure what a spirit tells me, but I trust them as they usually know how a person is going to respond to what they say.

Chris looked up and smiled at what Alan had just said. "That's Alan, always making a joke."

"Alan is telling me that even though you have a few scars on your face, nothing can mess up that handsome mug of yours! He says you're even sexier than before!"

Chris was smiling as tears streamed down his cheeks.

"Shut up, Alan!" he said out loud.

"Alan says you know he was always right in life and he for sure is always right now that he is in spirit."

"Alan, you were not always right," Chris replied.

I could tell that Chris was more comfortable during the reading now and Alan wanted to tease him.

"Alan is telling me that between you and him, he also had the better body, true?" I asked.

Smirking, Chris replied, "If his definition of a better body is that he was bigger in size, yes, but I am more cut than he could ever be."

"Alan says not anymore!" I said, as Alan joked with Chris. "Just one of the perks of being dead, he says, you can have any kind of body you want! He is also laughing and saying that it is usually easier for smaller guys like you to get into shape than it is for taller ones like him."

"He's not that much taller than me!" Chris quipped.

"He's bragging that being in heaven, you don't have to work out to have a great body and even though he doesn't have to exercise to keep in shape anymore, he still works out with you every single day."

Nodding his head, Chris said, "I feel him with me and it is hard to get through a routine without thinking about how much I miss him."

"He says you hear him pushing you to do more and more reps."

"I do and I also tell him to F-off."

We all started laughing at Chris's response. But I could tell by Alan's mood that he wanted to broach a more serious subject.

"Alan is mentioning something about you two not showing how much you loved each other in public. Does that make sense to you?"

"It does," Chris replied. "Even though we lived together, people just thought we were roommates, never expecting it was more than that."

"Well, he wants you to know that if he had it to do all over again, he would want the whole world to know how much you meant and continue to mean to him."

Chris started to tear up. "This was our last conversation in the car before we had the accident."

"Alan wants to know if you would do him a favor."

"Anything," Chris replied.

"He wants you to tell his family about the true relationship you both had."

Chris looked at me with fear in his eyes.

"God, telling his family was going to be hard enough to do with him, but by myself?"

"Alan says that you will not be by yourself, that he will be right beside you. He is telling me that his family thinks he never had a love in his life, and that by hiding who he was from them and what he had with you, he also took away the chance his family had to share in that love," I told him.

"I will have to think about that one," Chris replied.

"Alan is saying that he wants to be the one to get you to do this as he knows that it will help you as you continue moving forward with your life as well as in future relationships."

"I am not even thinking about another relationship at this point," Chris said, shaking his head with determination.

At that moment I could feel such great love and care from Alan to Chris.

"Alan understands this, but is saying that HE KNOWS what is up ahead for you and that in time you will feel different." I added, "To tell the truth, I am finding it funny that he keeps stressing the words I KNOW to you."

"That's because Alan always thought HE KNEW everything," Chris said with a grin. "If we had an argument, that was my usual go-to line, 'Oh you just know everything,' and he would say, 'I know I love you'...then Alan and I would laugh and we wouldn't even remember what the argument was about in the first place."

"Well, he definitely does know he loves you, he is telling me," I replied. "He is also talking about you watching a Brad Pitt movie."

Surprised, Chris responded, "I just watched it last night. I would always joke that he had the hots for Brad Pitt."

"He says don't pretend that you don't, too!"

Taking a deep breath, Chris replied, "Okay, I will admit it!"

"Doesn't matter, gay, straight, male, female...who doesn't have the hots for Brad Pitt!" I responded.

We all laughed.

Chris later told us that he did in fact meet with Alan's parents along with Alan's brother and sister-in-law, William and Sharon. Even though he was extremely nervous, he joined the family at the same restaurant where he had met up with William and Sharon the night the accident occurred. And after catching up with each other, with all the courage he had, Chris told the truth about the relationship that he and Alan shared.

Chris told me that even though William and Sharon were a little surprised with his announcement, what stunned them most was why Alan felt that he had to keep his being gay a secret. They told Chris they knew that Alan was kind of private about his personal life when it came to romance, but hoped that it was not because he thought he had to hide his sexuality from them. William even told Chris that he would sometimes say to Sharon, 'Wouldn't it be funny if Alan was actually gay?'

Alan's parents were a bit more shocked by the announcement. They both said that they had no idea their son was gay, and Alan's father even questioned how Alan could have hidden something like that from them, even making the comment that Alan did not "look or act" gay. Understanding how some perceive gay people, Chris, along with William and Sharon, explained to Alan's father that gay people do not necessarily have a certain look, or act in a certain manner to express their sexuality. They told Alan's parents that Alan was a perfect example of what it meant to be gay and defy description as to whom you are attracted. They wanted Alan's parents to understand that

Alan was still their son and his sexual preference didn't make him different from the young man they always loved.

Chris said that he heard from Alan's mother, who said that Alan's dad was starting to come to terms with their son's relationship with Chris and not too long after that, Alan's father even called Chris and invited him to watch a Miami Dolphins game at his home. Chris happily accepted.

6. Two for One

As Eleanor walked away from the gravesite, although her heart was heavy with sorrow, she knew that her beloved husband Joseph was no longer in pain. He'd fought a courageous battle against cancer for the last six months of his life but at the end, the cancer won and took the life of the man she loved. But Joseph did not fight this battle alone; Eleanor, too, was fighting right alongside him. From the day he was diagnosed with the terminal disease until the day she was at his bedside kissing him for the last time, Eleanor gave her heart and soul to make sure that his transition was peaceful and as painless as it could be.

But this was not the first time Eleanor had gone through such an experience.

Eleanor's first husband Frank had also gone through a similar passing, also being diagnosed with and passing from cancer. But the difference between the two was that Frank was given only six weeks to live.

Frank and Eleanor had quite a romance. She met him on a train going to New York City. She was meeting up with girl-friends for a two-day holiday in the city. It was Christmastime and she and her friends were going to do some shopping and try to catch a show. She hadn't seen them in years and was looking forward to visiting with her old friends again. She'd arrived just in time to board the train and struggled with her luggage. She lifted her overnight bag and attempted to place it in the overhead compartment. Seeing this young lady wrestling with the bulky item, the man seated next to her stood and helped her. She noticed how strikingly handsome he was, and how kind. He allowed her to sit next to the window. She smiled and accepted his graciousness. He introduced himself as Frank, an architect who was on his way to New York for business. Eleanor's father was in construction and the two hit it off instantly. By the time the train reached Penn Station, they had already made plans for dinner. Eleanor never did see her friends on that trip.

The couple married a year and a half later and their life was rich and rewarding.

Once Frank and Eleanor received the bad news from the doctors, they continued living their life the best they could with the cloud of death that hovered over Frank. He, never one to be discouraged, would joke with Eleanor that he hoped she would wait until he was cold in his grave before she started dating again. Though this would make Eleanor laugh, it would also make her angry. She would tell Frank to stop such talk. She was never going to marry again, as she would quip that husbands were just too much trouble. This would make Frank laugh even through the pain, but he would then promise her that he would do his best to pick out someone special for her once he was in Heaven. Eleanor would ask him why he thought he would even make it to Heaven, and he would tell her he knew he would because he had married an angel. Frank passed away exactly six weeks to the day of his diagnosis, one week shy of their thirty-fifth wedding anniversary.

Eleanor busied herself after Frank's passing with yard work and other chores. Every now and then a friend would invite her out for lunch or dinner, and she would go and enjoy catching up with them. A few years had passed after Frank was gone when on one of these outings something happened that she could never have even dreamed.

Eleanor met Joseph.

They met at a barbecue that a mutual friend was holding. Although she was not looking for love, it came to Eleanor and Joseph as a surprise, and the two married a few years later.

Life was good for both Eleanor and Joseph and the two would often refer back to Frank and hope that he was happy that the two were together. Eleanor would always remark to Joseph that she felt that it was Frank who brought them together in the first place. The two had been married for fourteen years, living life to the fullest, up until the day Joseph was given the bad news.

Eleanor could not believe this was happening to her again. She had gone through it once, but now found herself in the exact same position. Although she determined to be strong for Joseph, inside she was heartbroken that now both of her loves were to be taken away from her.

Six months came and went in the blink of an eye, and Eleanor again had to say goodbye to the man she loved.

———

When Eleanor came to see me, she was open to receiving messages from her husband, but had one question: Which one would come through?

Eleanor received her answer…

———

Eleanor came in and sat in front of me. She smiled, put her purse on the chair next to her and took a deep breath. I asked her who she would like me to connect with and she answered her husband.

When I began, I concentrated on Eleanor's husband, but what took me by surprise was that not only was there one husband that came, but two.

"Eleanor, I know you want me to connect with your husband, but for some reason, there are two gentlemen here. Do you have more than one husband in spirit?" I asked.

"Oh my, yes!" she exclaimed. "I didn't know who to ask for because I thought I might only be able to speak with one and did not want to offend the other."

I could hear both men laughing.

"Your husbands are laughing at you, Eleanor, and want you to know that it is okay, you don't have to choose just one. They're both going to speak!" I told her, laughing as well.

"I understand," she said, scratching her head. "Well, not really. I don't know how this is going to work," she stated, obviously confused.

"What do you mean?" I asked.

"I don't understand how it works in Heaven. I love both men and I don't want either one to be angry at me for doing so."

With that, I felt the love and compassion from both men toward their wife.

I smiled and said, "They want you to know that not only are they not angry with you, they both continue to love you!"

Eleanor let out a deep sigh of relief. It looked as if a weight had been taken off her shoulders.

I continued. "Husband number one, and I call him this because he is holding up one finger, telling me that he was your first husband, says that not only does he love you with all of his heart but he was the one that helped you find husband number two!"

"I knew it!" she said, slapping her leg with her hand. "I felt Frank had a hand in orchestrating my meeting Joseph! Before he passed, he used to joke about how he was going to steer the *right man to me, but I didn't really think he would, or if that was even possible."*

"Well, it is and he did!" I told her. "Frank also wants you to know that during your time together with Joseph, he knew you continued to make room in your heart for him, and that meant the world to him."

This put a smile on Eleanor's face.

"Frank also wants you to know that one of the first things that Joseph did when he reached the other side was to give Frank a hug and thank him for helping you two come together. So yes, both men are getting along just fine!" I assured her.

Relieved, she responded, "I was hoping to hear that!"

"Frank is telling me how you took care of him. He passed with cancer, correct?" I asked.

"Yes," Eleanor said, quietly.

At the same time I was telling Eleanor this, Joseph also let me feel the same way of passing.

"I am getting that Joseph did as well," I said. "He died of cancer also?"

"He did," she replied as she looked at the floor, shaking her head.

"Frank is telling me that this is also something they both had in common!"

"You tell Frank to behave himself, that's not funny," she said, trying to hold back a grin.

"Joseph is telling me how grateful he was to have you by his side during his illness. He knew you had gone through it

before with Frank, and how hard it was for you to go through it again. He also knew there was sadness behind your smile, a beautiful smile that would never leave your face," I conveyed to Eleanor.

With that Eleanor began to cry.

"I know there is a reason that God brought both of these wonderful men into my life, just like there is a reason for everything. Not a day goes by that I don't think of them both with love. I have always hoped that they were getting along," she said.

I smiled at her and said, "Again, they very much get along! The one thing that makes both men the happiest is that you still love them as much as they love you. They want you to know that you never have to feel guilty, as, being in spirit, they understand how it is possible to love more than one person the way you do."

"I was wondering if there would be some jealousy between the two," she stated with a look of concern.

Hearing that question, I took a few moments for the answer to come.

"Frank tells me that there is absolutely no jealousy between the two. They both understand the importance of you being able to give your love to someone; it is who you are. And they are happy that this is something you continue to give them both, every day," I relayed. "So from this day forward, always remember that you have two husbands by your side, loving you and taking care of you, just as you did for both of them."

Tears started to stream down Eleanor's cheeks as she finally was able to receive the answer to a question that had been of great concern to her for quite some time. She now understood that she continued to have the love of both men that meant so much to her in life, men who would cherish her always.

I continued. "Eleanor, do you have a cat? Frank is saying something about teasing a cat."

Surprised, Eleanor replied, "I do! I just got her a couple of months ago."

"Frank says for you to take notice of your cat looking up at him. He says that he waves his hand in front of her face and makes your cat respond by looking up," I told her.

Eleanor responded, excitedly, "I have noticed Custard looking up at nothing!"

With that, Joseph joked, "Frank is laughing and saying, how dare you call him nothing!"

Laughing, Eleanor replied, "He knows what I mean! Tell him from now on, I will know who Custard is watching."

I smiled. "Joseph is laughing at the name Custard, by the way," I added.

"I like the name Custard!" Eleanor shot back. "It took me a week to come up with a name. I tried out several different ones and then Custard just came to me."

"And guess why it came to you?" I asked.

"Why?" she asked.

"Because Joseph is the one who gave you the name! He says that you were having such trouble naming your cat that he came up with it and gave it to you through thought!" I told her.

"*Through thought?*"

"*Yes, this is one of many ways that a spirit will use to communicate with you. They want you to know that you do hear both men in your head all the time; it is just that you don't realize it is them.*"

"*I am so happy to hear that!*" she said. "*I was sitting with Custard and wondering what I should call her. I wanted her name to be just right. She has such a beautiful color, sort of a cream, and the name Custard just came to me!*"

I told her, "And now you know why."

Then I took a moment as I watched Joseph showing me something he was holding in his hand. It was blurry at first, and then I was able to focus on it and understood what it was ... another cat.

"*Joseph is holding a cat, one that is in spirit. But he places it next to the one you have. Did your cat's mother pass?*"

She cried, "She did! I got Custard from a rescue shelter. Apparently Custard's mother was killed by a car and Custard was found nearby."

"*Know that Custard's mother is just fine in spirit and will also continue to look after her baby. By the way, Joseph says that Custard's mother is happy that you have adopted her kitten,*" I explained.

This brought another big smile to Eleanor's face.

As the reading progressed, both Joseph and Frank continued to take turns talking with Eleanor and sharing their memories and observations. And as the reading was coming to an end, Eleanor had one more problem on her mind.

"Is it okay to ask one last question?" Eleanor asked.

"Feel free to ask," I replied.

"I know that this may sound silly, but when it is my turn to be in Heaven, who will be my husband?"

I again took a moment to see what either spirit would have to say.

"Both of your husbands are laughing and Frank wants you to know that you don't have to ever ponder that question. He says even though it is hard to explain, he wants you to know that everything always works its way out in Heaven, and he can promise you that!" I said.

Relief softened Eleanor's face.

I continued. "Joseph is also adding that since you are only in your seventies, you still have plenty of time to add another husband to your list!"

Eleanor rolled her eyes and replied, "Two was more than enough, thank you!" She added, "I think I will be content with the two I already had."

"You mean have," I replied.

"Yes, have," Eleanor responded, holding her hand to her heart.

———

Eleanor thanked me after her reading and said that she was very happy to have that weight off of her shoulders. Believing in an afterlife, she always knew that both husbands would meet each other in spirit, but was not sure how they would act toward one another. Having both men come through with messages for her together made her realize that she did not have to choose one over another and that it was all right to continue to love them both. She was still unsure how it would work when it was her turn to be in spirit, but understood that Heaven has a way of making everything right.

7. HEAVENLY MATCHMAKER

———

Tracy was always into motorcycles—how could she not be? Her father, Vinny, was a lifelong biker. Vinny used to take Tracy on his bike to show her off to their family and friends. He had a special side car that her mom and she would ride in. Tracy's mother never worried when father and daughter took a trip together, as she knew her husband drove safely and that Tracy was the apple of his eye.

As Tracy grew up, she shared her love for motorcycles with her father. This was something they had in common and the two would always try to outdo the other with their knowledge of bikes. When she became old enough to ride on her own, he bought her one for her very own. The family would take long rides together on the open road. This made them a close-knit and loving family.

On Tracy's twenty-first birthday, Vinny surprised her with a road trip to Sturgis, South Dakota. Every year, Sturgis has a

major motorcycle rally where bikers come to express their enthu-
siasm for motorcycles. Tracy and her dad rode down the main
drag with their bikes and her pop couldn't be prouder when
they would run into his friends. They couldn't believe the little
girl in the side car had grown up to be such a beautiful young
girl. Tracy had a great time with her father and they decided
to stop for lunch at a local restaurant before heading out. It was
their last day there and she hated for it to end. While eating, she
kept staring at a young man a few tables down. Vinny noticed
that she hadn't touched her food. He saw her stealing glances
at the young man and that he was doing the same to her. He
smiled and whispered, "You might as well go say hello; didn't I
teach you to take the bull by the horns?" She was embarrassed
that her father had caught her, but he was right. She marched
over to the table of young men and stared right at the young
man. To her, the others at the table didn't even exist. She in-
troduced herself and he stood and introduced himself. His name
was Jimmy. Jimmy had just graduated from college and was
attending the rally with some of his friends. Tracy knew that
they were about to leave and looked to her father. He called the
two over to the table and once introductions were made, he told
Tracy that his bike might need to be checked out before the trip
back. He asked Jimmy if he would keep his daughter company
until he returned. Delighted, Jimmy told his friends he would
catch up with them later. Jimmy and Tracy sat at the table for
hours, drinking coffee and talking about everything under the
sun. Jimmy reminded Tracy so much of her father, minus the

long hair and tattoos. The two hit it off instantly and kept in contact after the rally.

After several months of having a long-distance relationship, Tracy and Jimmy couldn't stand living apart anymore. Jimmy had landed a good job in Las Vegas and wanted her to come join him. Tracy got on her bike, kissed her mother and father goodbye, and headed to Las Vegas, where she and Jimmy continued their relationship. Six months later, they married.

As the years went by, the two became a family of five with three wonderful children that Tracy and Jimmy loved very much.

Life was good for the two. That was until one day when Tracy found her beloved husband at home, dead.

After her husband's passing, Tracy decided to move back to her hometown. She thought it would be good for her children to be close to her family, and she needed the support she was receiving from her parents.

A few years after Tracy moved back, something happened without warning. Tracy fell in love again.

Tracy came to me for a reading with mixed emotions. Being a widow for three years, she never thought she would fall in love again…but somehow it happened and she felt guilty for having these feelings. She loved the man she was now with, but continued to love Jimmy and this was tearing her up inside.

———

"Who would you like me to try to connect with today?" I asked.

Tracy replied, "My husband."

I told her, "I am happy you said that because there is a husband coming through to me and he's telling me that he has a few things on his mind!"

"That sounds like him," she said with a worried smile. "He always had a few things on his mind."

"What I do, Tracy, is ask them if they would like to communicate the way that they passed to me, and they will do this by letting me experience it," I said.

At that moment her husband started to send me a sharp pain around my head area and then snapped his fingers at me, meaning it was a quick passing.

"Your husband is giving me pain in my head; did he pass quickly of head trauma or a brain aneurism?" I asked.

"Yes, he did, it was an aneurism," Tracy replied, as she started to cry. "I came home one day from work and found Jimmy dead on the floor. He was such a strong healthy man and only fifty-five years old. It was totally unexpected."

"I can also tell Jimmy has a sense of humor, as he is telling me to say that if you thought it was unexpected, how do you think it was for him?!"

Tracy started to laugh though her tears. "That's my Jimmy; he always knew how to put a smile on my face!"

"He still does. He wants you to know that he is, however, very sorry for the way you had to find him," I added.

Of course, when I heard and relayed this message from Jimmy, I assumed he was sorry for Tracy having to find his body, but that wasn't it, as he started laughing as he said it.

I make it a rule not to censor messages from a spirit, or even how they relay them to me. At that moment I was thinking to myself how odd it was for Jimmy to be laughing when discussing such a delicate matter and certainly the traumatic experience Tracy must have had. So by him laughing while giving this message, I had no choice but to think that something humorous must have happened. I hoped that this was the case, anyway.

"Tracy, I'm sorry, but for some reason Jimmy is now laughing about the way you found him," I ventured, unsure of her response. "Was there something funny about it?"

Tracy too started to smile again. "I found Jimmy in the bathroom next to the toilet. I had no alternative but to leave him there until the paramedics came," she said.

"Jimmy is saying that even though it was not the most dignified way to pass over… at least he flushed first."

With that she laughed out loud, and I too started to laugh along with Tracy and Jimmy.

More confirmations came through as our conversation continued. Jimmy talked about how proud he was of Tracy and the kids, how well she was doing, and how he was still very much a part of her life. I could tell these two people meant a great deal to each other, not only by their words, but by the deep love I could feel coming through from both of them… true soul mates.

It was at that time that Jimmy brought up the subject of Tracy and another man. I am usually cautious if this happens as I don't want to upset the person being read if they are not seeing someone or if they are not open to that idea.

"Tracy. Hmmm, how to say this.... Jimmy is talking about you and another man and he shows me a heart with this, are you seeing someone else at this time?"

Tracy became silent before she gave me her reply. "Yes." And with that, she broke down and started to cry.

She continued, "I wasn't looking for love again, but it just happened. I met Jerry almost a year ago at a mall while I was looking for a present for a family member. He too was looking at the same item and we struck up a conversation. One thing led to the next and we started going out. I never considered it dating as we both just wanted some companionship. But the more we saw of each other, the more our feelings grew for each other. And I don't know what to do as I still love Jimmy. I feel so guilty!"

With that I could tell by Jimmy's emotions of compassion and love that he wanted to help his distraught wife.

I said, "With much care, Jimmy wants to convey that he knows how much you love him, as your love is a part of his soul. He also wants you to know how much he loves you too ... this will never change. But one of his greatest desires is for you to be happy."

A flicker of a smile came across Tracy's face through her tears.

"It always has been," she said. "He would always tell me, Daddy ain't happy unless Mama is happy."

I continued. "But he wants you to know that meeting Jerry and falling in love with him does not take away from the love you have for him."

With a sigh, she answered, "That is true. I do and I always will love him."

"He is also telling me that he is the one that directed you to meet Jerry."

Tracy asked, puzzled, "He did?"

"Yes. Jimmy is mentioning the present you went to buy when you met this man."

"Yes, it was my sister's birthday and I wanted to give her something unique. I kept thinking and thinking about what to give her and as the date grew closer, I was running out of time. As I went window shopping in a mall and still had no luck, I suddenly got an idea. I wanted to see if I could find my sister a remote control with large numbers on it. I had seen them in catalogs and thought she might appreciate not having to search for her glasses every time she wanted to watch TV."

"That certainly was a unique gift, but where do you think that 'idea' came from to buy it?"

"Jimmy?"

"That's what he is telling me! By giving you this 'thought out of nowhere' to buy the remote control, he put you on the path that led you to meeting this new man."

"*Wow, I am so relieved to know he had a hand in this,*" *Tracy replied.*

"*Of course, Jimmy could only place you on a certain path; it was and is up to you how the developments will evolve with Jerry. But Jimmy tells me that he likes Jerry and that you know how to handle him,*" *I relayed to her.*

Tracy's eyes sparkled at learning that not only was Jimmy still with her, but how important her happiness was to him. That her joy was his joy in heaven.

I said, "By the way, for some reason Jimmy is laughing again and calling Jerry your 'Boy Toy.' Do you understand this?"

"*Boy Toy!*" *Tracy said with a laugh. "He's only five years younger than me!*"

I replied, "Well, if you want to be a cradle robber that is certainly up to you!"

We all laughed with that as the reading came to its conclusion.

———

One of the most common struggles widowed people have is whether or not to allow themselves to have another relationship with someone new.

I have spoken to a lot of widows and widowers and there is no right or wrong answer to this situation as each is different.

There are those who have had a long relationship with a spouse and once one of them passes over, the other is content to live alone while cherishing the memories they have of that relationship.

And there are others who were equally in love with someone who passes, but feel they still have more to give to someone else. But sometimes when this happens, that person may experience mixed emotions as if they are somehow cheating on or even disrespecting their previous mate.

And there are the other times when someone is not seeking love, but it seems to come out of nowhere …

There should never be guilt when falling in love again after the passing of a spouse. Love is from God and it is the best gift we can give as well as receive. As in the above situation, you never know what that spouse in spirit may have in store for you!

8. Wedding Sorrows

———

They had been predicting rain all week for the day Elizabeth and Tom were to be married. But when Elizabeth awoke that morning, the sun was shining brightly, and even though it is considered a good omen for it to be raining on your wedding day, she was happy that it had not.

The day had come faster than she could ever have imagined, and although it took a year to plan, the time flew by. And even though this was the happiest day of Elizabeth's life, she also felt a little sad inside, perhaps because she had not really enjoyed the process of preparing for this special day. Thinking back now, she realized that the planning had been some of the most memorable parts of the process.

She remembered dragging Tom to choose the flowers, which became quite an event. When they first entered the florist's shop, he saw a batch of sunflowers and told her they were perfect and that with just a few bunches of those around the church, they were set. She told him he was not going to get out of this that easily and they sat for two hours looking at every type of hydrangea and rose until they agreed on the right colors and textures.

Then there was the food tasting. Tom thought a hamburger and hotdog feast for the afternoon might be great for all the guests, but when they both tasted the filet and chicken with the Cajun theme, they both agreed that this was the caterer for them. Elizabeth chuckled as she thought back on the cake tasting experience, as well. This was what Tom was looking forward to the most. Tom pretended that he didn't know what cake he wanted and asked to sample everything the baker had. She brought out a large assortment of cakes and icings and he cleaned every crumb on the plate. Elizabeth laughed under her breath as she kicked Tom under the table when he was about to ask for seconds. She decided the cake would be red velvet, but his favorite was lemon. The baker solved the problem by telling them Elizabeth could have the red velvet and Tom's groom cake could be lemon. And even though the planning of their wedding had been stressful, thinking back, she realized it was a wonderful experience.

But as Elizabeth got up from bed the morning of her wedding, she shook off any pesky negative emotions and thought about the one thing that made her the happiest woman in the world: Today she was going to marry her love, Tom!

She and Tom first met when they were in high school. He was a junior, she a sophomore and the two were in Drama Club together. She had noticed him from afar, but she didn't think he knew she existed. So when the time came, Elizabeth decided to audition for the school play and at the audition, her heart was in her throat because Tom too was auditioning. Elizabeth gave the audition of a lifetime and to her surprise and excitement, she and Tom were both cast in the production of Beauty and the Beast. She was playing the part of Belle, and Tom playing the part of the Beast.

Tom was made for this role. He was on the football team and built like a brick wall; some had even given him the nickname, the beast. And although he was happy to get the lead role, Tom told the drama teacher that football had to come first, and asked if they would work around his schedule and games in order for him to find the time to rehearse. It was all worked out and Elizabeth was excited that maybe Tom would now be able to get to know who she was. And did he ever!

Elizabeth was nervous about the first rehearsal, but there was no need for worry as she and Tom hit it off right from the start. And as they practiced the play every day, Tom and Elizabeth became closer and closer. Tom loved to show off his strength by sweeping Elizabeth off of her feet and swinging her around the stage growling like a beast. It was during this special time that Elizabeth knew that Tom was one day going to be her husband.

The play was a huge success and the two continued their romance throughout their high school years and even college.

After college, Tom decided to enlist to become a Marine. This was something his father had done and he felt it was important to continue in his family tradition. Elizabeth was sad to see him deployed but had always known this was something he had his heart set on. She also knew that the day would come when Tom would come home and they would be married. Today was that day.

Elizabeth met her best friend at the church that morning to make sure all of the planning of the past year was in order. She wanted this day to be perfect for her and Tom, and go off without a hitch. She and Tom had decided that they were going to have an afternoon wedding so that their guests could then relax afterward at the dinner reception and party the night away. She was second guessing the fast-approaching afternoon timeline, as it gave her less time to wrap up the preparations, but she did not want to further delay the day she would marry the love of her life.

Most of Elizabeth's bridesmaids had also arrived early. All the girls gathered in the back of the church where they were able to start getting ready for the big ceremony. As Elizabeth was having her hair done, her phone rang and it was Tom on the other end. Tom laughed at Elizabeth, telling her that she got to the church way too early and that he was just getting out of bed. Elizabeth told Tom that it was typical for him to be so relaxed and that he better not be late for their big day. Tom made a joke pretending to have forgotten that it was that day, and Elizabeth told him that she was going to make sure that he was never going to forget it again. Tom told her that he knew the only thing he would never forget was that he loved her with all his heart. She smiled and kissed the phone. He told Elizabeth that he had better get up and shower and that he was going to see her soon.

———

As the day went on, all the bridesmaids and Elizabeth were giddy with excitement, and while Elizabeth was having her makeup done, her phone rang again. This time she received a call from Tom's father. And what Elizabeth heard made her go completely numb and turn as white as the wedding dress she was preparing to put on. Tom's father could barely speak. Tom's father told Elizabeth that there had been a terrible accident. Tom was on his way to his best man's house when his car hit a tree. Tom passed away instantly. The news of Tom's death tore Elizabeth apart. She dropped the phone as everyone in the room stood silent, staring at her. Elizabeth screamed, "Tom is dead!"

Elizabeth fell to the floor on top of her wedding dress, the symbol of the love she and Tom had shared. She was sobbing, crying into the dress that was now just a crumpled mess on the floor. Elizabeth thought, How could it be that the happiest day of my life has now turned into the worst day of my life? How could Tom have served his country overseas and come home without a scratch, only to end up being killed on his wedding day?

How?

———

When Elizabeth came to see me, along with one of her friends, Terri, she was still experiencing overwhelming grief. It had been about nine months since Tom's passing and Terri thought there may be a chance to help Elizabeth heal if she were to hear from Tom.

Terri was right. Tom had a lot to tell his love Elizabeth…

———

"*I can already tell you that your fiancé is here. He seems to be a big guy physically, and his personality is just as big," I said.*

Elizabeth started to cry and Terri put her arm around her shoulders.

"*Yes," Elizabeth answered quietly.*

I continued. "Tom wants you to know that he feels all the pain that you have been going through since his passing and he has been with you every day since then."

Elizabeth said through her tears, "My heart is broken. I just don't understand why it happened." She balled the tissues in her hand into a wad.

I asked Tom what she meant. I assumed she was referring to his passing and asked him if he could relay that to me. Tom then started showing me a picture in my mind of a car in an accident.

"*Was Tom in an automobile accident? He is showing me that," I asked Elizabeth.*

"Yes! Yes he was! And I don't understand why it happened, especially that day!"

At that exact moment, I heard Tom tell me, "wedding," so I asked, "Did Tom pass on your wedding day or your anniversary?"

Elizabeth started to sob harder while Terri took both of her hands in her own and started to rub them.

"Yes," was the only word Elizabeth could manage to say.

When I am giving messages like this, there are several things I am experiencing at the same time. Not only do I see the emotions of the person I am giving the messages to, but I can feel them as well. I could feel how much Elizabeth had been suffering and understood why she had been in such pain. This day was supposed to be the happiest of her life, the day most women have dreamed of since they were little girls, and it was taken away from Elizabeth in an instant.

But at the same time I was feeling her pain, I was also linked into Tom, and could feel his emotions as well. The difference between the two was that although Tom's heart too was heavy for what his love Elizabeth was going through, I also could feel his compassion and confidence in knowing the reasons why.

"Tom is telling me that this was an accident and that there was no one else involved."

Elizabeth looked straight at me with sorrowful eyes and stated, "That's what we don't understand. What happened?"

I said, "Let me see if Tom can tell us."

Again, silently, I asked Tom if he could tell me how the accident took place.

"Tom is telling me that a dog ran across the road and when he swerved to avoid it, he lost control of his car."

Elizabeth gasped and shouted, "I knew it, that's what we felt happened!" With this, Elizabeth put her head down and cried again. But now there was some relief as Elizabeth had some answers about this horrific occurrence.

As I looked at Elizabeth, I saw Tom rubbing her shoulders and stroking her hair. I told Elizabeth what Tom was doing and it seemed that she could feel his touch.

"Tom wants you to know that his love for you did not die the day he did, because he is in fact not dead," I said.

Elizabeth nodded as she wiped her tears.

I continued. "Tom wants me to relay to you that it is impossible for you or any of his family members and friends to understand why he passed away that day the way he did, but please know that it was his time to be in spirit."

An agitated Elizabeth responded, "How could it be his time to be in spirit?" Elizabeth spat out angrily, "He was so young, and we had our whole future ahead of us. How could God have taken him away from me?" She sat back in her chair stiffly.

I could feel Tom's compassion for Elizabeth. "Tom understands how you feel; he would be feeling the same way if the situation were reversed. But in spirit, all of these questions are answered and you realize why things happen when they do. He wants you to know that he is not oblivious to what you and his family and friends have been going through, as he has been a part of that every day, going through it with you. He also knows how angry you have been at God, and honestly he doesn't blame you . . . he understands, and God too understands. And anger is part of the process."

"What process?" she asked, puzzled.

"The process that is necessary for your soul to grow. As you, his family and his friends, all of you, experience his passing, you will also experience a change and a difference in each and every one of your lives, and your soul will mature and gain strength from this life event.

"Tom wants you to understand that all of the negative feelings you have are natural, but once the anger and negative emotions start to fade, and they will fade, what you will be left with is the most important feeling that you will ever have, love."

Elizabeth asked, "When did he become so smart about all of this stuff?"

"Tom says it's another perk that you get being in spirit, baby."

This made Elizabeth smile.

When giving a reading where there are so many unanswered questions involved, I experience the situation of the reading in many ways. I feel for the person I am giving the reading to as I can feel their pain when they are pleading to God to give them the reason why. But I also feel what the spirit is feeling, as there is a confidence within them that comes with knowing the answers to all the whys, and what their life and subsequent passing mean.

With that, a spirit will try to convey their compassionate confidence to their loved ones here, but although they may not be able to express it in words, they will reassure them that there is a reason for everything and one day, they, too, will have all the answers.

———

"Tom is telling me that what will help you is to continue to move forward with your life."

"Forward how?" she asked, with weariness in her voice.

"He wants you to know that you have so much to look forward to! He knows that you keep thinking about the past, and not your future, and this is keeping you from the great things that he sees are in your future. He says that although he wants you to always remember the time that you two had together, and to keep those memories in your heart as he does in his, realize that there is much more for you ahead."

I could tell Tom wanted to steer the conversation toward Elizabeth's future and I could sense by his emotions where he was going next…

I took a deep breath and told her, "Tom wants you to know that even though you may not want to hear this now, you will be finding another love."

Elizabeth started to weep again.

"Tom was the only love I've ever known," she replied.

"He wants you to be open to a new relationship because, while it may seem that your life is over, it has really only just begun."

Through tears, shaking her head, Elizabeth replied, "I just don't see that happening."

Smiling, I said, "But Tom does see it happening. Again, he says that being in spirit has a few perks and one is that he is able to see the future. He already knows that you are going to be able to move forward and that there is going to be another special person coming into your life."

I could tell that Elizabeth started to consider the idea. But she responded with, "I don't know if I will ever be ready to love someone like I loved Tom."

"He is telling me you will and that it may even happen sooner than you think. He is saying that he has been working overtime for you!"

Elizabeth laughed out loud for the first time. "Oh, my god! Tom would always say that to me! Girl, you keep me working overtime!" Her best friend Terri gripped her hand again.

"He still is, Elizabeth, and Tom wants you to know that he is and will always be a part of your life. His love for you did not die the day of the accident and it has only grown stronger. And he promises that when you do find your next love, he will still continue to love you the way he does today, as he knows you will do the same for him."

"I will. I will love Tom forever," Elizabeth declared resolutely.

"Tom says you're ready to move forward and he will be moving forward with you every step of the way."

More at ease and confident, Elizabeth said, "I hope so. I need all the help he can give me."

"Tom says that you can always count on him, he is always going to be your beast."

"Oh my God! I can't believe you said that!" Elizabeth gasped. "That is how we met; we were in a school play together!"

"Well, it is a wonderful confirmation that this beast is going to always protect his beauty…"

———

Elizabeth did in fact fall in love and she and her husband have two children. She told me that she met her husband not long after her first reading with me and that she didn't know that finding him was going to happen so fast, just as Tom had told her. Elizabeth also said that she could still feel Tom with her and knew that he was true to his promise of keeping his eye on her, always.

9. Never Too Late

Nicky was a bright girl who loved to dream big. As a toddler, she would dress up as a princess and tell her parents how when she was older, like eight years old, she was going to marry a prince and live in a big beautiful castle, just like the ones in the books her mother would read to her. She told them not to worry, they could live there too.

As she grew, Nicky continued her dreams and would talk about marrying her favorite boy in a band or whatever teen idol was hot at that time. Her parents would encourage her, saying that anything is possible.

As Nicky approached her mid-teen years, she was starting to not just talk about boys and romance, but act on her feelings by going on dates. Of course no parent is ready for this, but hers considered Nicky mature enough and said their little girl was growing up.

Autumn was in full swing and the homecoming dance was to take place in a few weeks. Nicky was excited about attending. She had been asked to the dance by a very cute boy who was in one of her classes, one that her parents knew, and they too started becoming just as excited about this date as Nicky was. How could they not, as it was the only thing Nicky had been talking about for weeks.

About a week before the big event, Nicky and some of her friends were walking home from school on a beautiful fall day. The sun was shining brightly through the beautiful colored leaves on the trees and a chilly breeze put just enough nip in the air for Nicky and her pals to wear their coats.

The kids decided to cut through some woods that were close to the school. It was not the easiest way home, but it was the fastest. As they walked, they had to cross a creek with large rocks going across it, that were used as stepping stones to get to the other side. Usually the kids around the area easily did this. But this time, after a heavy rain, the creek had swollen just enough that the water was now much higher and the stones were barely above water level.

Nicky and her friends thought about turning around, but they had come this far and were anxious to get home. So they decided to go ahead and cross the stream anyway. Nicky was the last of her friends to make that journey across and for whatever reason, her feet slipped out from underneath her and she fell into the rapid-moving current.

The unthinkable happened and Nicky drowned that day at the age of fifteen.

Nicky's parents Karen and Larry came to me to connect with their daughter, and although my heart goes out to everyone in need of my help in contacting a loved one in spirit, the reading takes just a little more heart when it involves a child.

Nicky connected to me quickly with a strong feeling of love for her parents. She was very energetic and after a few minutes of discussion about her passing and how much she loved her parents, and assurance that she was helping them in their lives, she changed the subject to something her parents were having a hard time accepting.

"Nicky is telling me that she liked to dance and still does!" I said.

"Oh yes, she did," replied Karen, who now became more animated.

"She was always in her room dancing around, sometimes with her friends and sometimes just by herself. We would peek inside the door and she would yell at us when she caught us," Larry said, with a small smile on his face.

"Well, don't you worry!" I said. "She wants you to know that she is still dancing away in her room, but it is a lot harder for you to catch her doing it now!"

They laughed. "We have kept her room exactly as she left it, posters hanging on the wall and all," Karen affirmed.

"Nicky is begging you now not to tell me what posters those are! But why do I have a feeling there may be some Justin Bieber pictures there?" I asked.

Both parents laughed and I could feel the mood of the two had lifted when speaking of the things Nicky loved so much. Larry replied, "Don't get mad at us, Nicky, we're not the ones who told him!"

I could hear Nicky laughing at that remark and I conveyed her next thought. "Nicky says that her crush was good at the time, but she has grown up a little since then."

"Really?" asked Karen. "Do spirits grow in Heaven?"

"They can if they want," I said. "This is one of those areas where it is hard to comprehend how it works there. Young people can grow older and older people can become young again, with anything in between. Most of the time a spirit will come to me at the age that they have passed into spirit as a reference for me and the one receiving a reading to confirm that I am connecting to the right person. But it is always up to the spirit as to what they want to do."

"I never thought about it like that," Larry said, sitting up.

"Well, Nicky is telling me something and this is why she directed the conversation in this direction. She says that she has aged just a couple of years now and that you have been celebrating her birthday each year."

"Yes, we always commemorate her birthday by buying a cake."

"She appreciates that and wants you to know that she has indeed grown older as each year progressed, but that is not all she wants you to know."

I paused to concentrate on the next message that Nicky had to convey to her parents as I could tell by her emotions that this was something that had been troubling both of them.

I continued. "Speaking of dancing, Nicky is telling me about a dance and she is giving me the feeling that you have been sad about it, does that make any sense to you?"

Her parents fell silent at that moment as Karen began to cry. Larry took Karen's hand and held it tightly.

Karen replied through her tears, "Nicky was about to go to her first dance before she died."

Larry took over. "This was something she had been looking forward to, and I just can't believe that she never got to go."

Again, I took a moment to concentrate on Nicky's reply. I could tell she was about to explain something that she had been wanting her parents to know for a long time.

"Nicky confirms that she did in fact go to the dance."

"What?" asked Karen.

"Nicky says that not only was she able to go to the dance, she even wore the dress you bought for her!"

This gave Larry tears as well. "I picked up the dress she wanted to wear the day she died."

"She wants you to know that it's not just hanging unused in her closet but that she wore the same dress to her dance."

The two became speechless as I continued.

"Nicky is telling me that you have to understand that being in spirit, not only was she able to go to the dance that night, she was also with you."

Karen exclaimed, "I thought I felt her with us that night."

I continued. "You did! And this is why she is confirming it for you. But she also is telling me that part of the sadness you were feeling that night is because you felt that she not only missed out on the dance, but other dances and experiences that teens have here. Nicky wants you to know that this is not true at all!"

"How's that?" Larry asked.

"Nicky is still very much alive and, you could say, 'growing up.' Even though she is in spirit and knows a lot more about what this life is about, she still gets to enjoy all that any teenager does here. Not only is she able to watch her friends and enjoy their company while they are doing their activities, but she wants you to know that she gets to do the same activities in her spirit life."

"I never thought of that," Larry said.

"And this is why she is excited to be telling you this and hopes to help you understand that she has continued to live her life, not only while loving and taking care of you both, but also by being able to do the things that kids her age do."

Karen replied, "We have been heartbroken that Nicky was not only unable to experience her first dance, but also her first date, her first kiss, the whole growing up process. When it was time for her to go to her first dance, around the time she had passed, we thought like many parents how fast our child was growing up and we would have given anything to turn back time. It's hard to watch your children grow up so quickly.

But after her passing, we found that we missed even more moments that were to never occur."

I affirmed, *"Now you know that they are occurring. And Nicky knows how much you would have loved to share these moments in her life, but she hopes that even though you may not be aware of this, she is in fact experiencing such events in her life!"*

Karen sighed and squeezed Larry's hand. I could see by Larry and Karen's expressions that this did help to lighten some of the burden they had both been carrying.

Larry responded, "This does bring us some comfort. We wanted more than anything on this Earth for Nicky not to have died. She was our world and it broke our hearts that having passed so young, she didn't get the chance to really start living."

"Nicky wants you to know that not only is she living her life, but she—"

Nicky started adding to what she had just said, but I could tell that she was a little hesitant to relay this next message. Spirits are usually not like this, so I was alerted that the next subject was going to be important.

"What? What is it?" Larry asked.

"Nicky is telling me that she has a boyfriend—"

"What!" Larry interjected, just as any father would.

"This is what she is telling me. Nicky wants you to know that she has met a boy her own age in spirit that she, well, let's just say, likes him very much!"

Karen was now crying, but this time, with happiness.

"Nicky says that she was introduced to him by some of her friends."

"Friends?"

I repeated Nicky's response. "Yes, of course, Dad! We make friends here too, you know!"

"I don't know why, but I never thought of them making friends up there, much less having boyfriends!" Karen quipped, smiling.

"They do, and she has," I answered. "Nicky says that you would both like him and that he laughs at all of her jokes."

"Nicky was always quick witted," Frank added.

"She still is, and is telling me that you don't have to worry, she is still your little girl, Dad, and that she would never do anything you would not approve."

Tears started to stream from Larry's eyes. "She is my little girl," said Larry, wiping away the tears. "I love her so much and I miss her every minute of the day."

With that, we all started tearing up.

"Nicky loves you both and knows how much you miss her. But she wants you to know that there is not a day that goes by when she is not with you. She is holding up her index finger and wants you to know that taking care of her mom and dad is her number one priority!"

"She would always hold up her finger and tell us we were number one!"

"You still are, and will always be," I agreed.

Larry regained his composure and asked, "Now what about this boy?"

We all laughed at Larry's question, even Nicky.

"She wants you to know that he reminds her a lot of her dad."

"Right answer," Larry replied, smiling.

"And by the way, she says, don't forget that her grandparents keep an eye on her as well!"

"That was my next question," Karen remarked.

"Nicky is asking me to tell you to not keep pressing on them to watch her so carefully, she does need her 'space' as well." She told me this, laughing.

"Something she would always tell us!" Larry said. "Tell her she's got it!"

———

Both Larry and Karen left having the confirmation that their beautiful daughter Nicky was not only still alive and well, but she was in fact still growing up.

Just as in this life, life in spirit does not stand still. Spirits not only continue to grow spiritually, but continue to live their life by doing the same things they would be doing in this physical world such as enjoying friendships and even finding love.

10. Heavenly Tattoo

A sweet mature woman named Millie came to me for a reading in hopes that I would connect with her husband Sam, who had passed away of natural causes in his eighties.

Millie met Sam back in the 1970s when she worked as an airline stewardess. Sam was on one of her flights and the two struck up a conversation. Sam was a real estate developer and often flew around the country scouting out properties for his business. Though Millie was always nice to the passengers onboard her plane, there was just something special about Sam that Millie couldn't shake. Before the flight ended, Sam asked Millie if she would be interested in perhaps getting together sometime for dinner. Though Millie made it a rule not to become involved with any of her passengers, she felt that this was the one time it was right to break her own rule.

The two met for dinner, which turned into many dinners, which eventually led to many dates and finally marriage.

Both Millie and Sam were madly in love with each other and enjoyed their life together. Millie continued to work as a stewardess and Sam would always book his flights in tandem with Millie's work schedule.

And even though the two of them never had children, their immediate families and friends kept them busy.

As time went by and the two grew older, their love for each other only grew stronger.

One Christmas, the two decided to be adventurous and spend the time away from home. They had always spent the holidays at home but with all the nieces and nephews grown and friends having their own celebrations, the couple decided that this was the year to get away. Although the two of them would travel often, they had always wanted to spend the holidays in Hawaii, a place they had never had a chance to visit before.

Hawaii was beautiful and a tropical Christmas was magical. The couple spent Christmas Eve under the stars sitting on the deck toasting each other and reminiscing. They exchanged small gifts and it was time for bed. Waking up the next morning, they saw it would be a glorious Christmas day and the weather in Hawaii could not have been better. The sun was coming up and a warm breeze made taking a walk on the beach all the more tempting. Sam and Millie put on some comfortable clothes, took each other by the hand and made their way to their secluded beach. As the two drank in the beauty of their location, Millie all of a sudden felt Sam's grasp *on her hand become stronger. At first she thought he was just playing around but when his grip started to hurt her, she watched as he dropped to the ground. Sam had died.*

————

Millie was anxious for the reading to get started and I could immediately feel Sam connect to me as I opened myself up for communication. I could tell that he was ready for me to start giving out his messages.

"Millie, Sam is here and though I can only say the words, he wants you to know how much he loves you!" I told her.

Millie started to tear up.

"Sam also wants you to know that he KNOWS how much you love him and that your love is a part of his very soul. But it always has been, he says."

Touching her heart, Millie replied, "And his is a part of mine."

When I conduct a reading, there are a few images and feelings I will try to have a spirit relay to me, not only for confirmation, but to also experience what some people might consider a negative, and that is the way the spirit passes. If a spirit wants to convey this to me, the best way is by letting me feel what they felt at the time of their passing. By receiving this, I can identify it and understand the cause. I say, "if a spirit wants," as it is always up to the spirit what they will bring through in a reading. They do this by showing, telling or even letting me "feel" what they did.

I quietly asked Sam how he passed, and I started to feel pressure in my heart area.

"Millie, did Sam pass with a heart attack?" I asked.

"Yes, he did," Millie replied, teary eyed.

"I can tell you by the way he is expressing it that he passed very quickly."

Looking down, Millie affirmed, "Yes, very quickly."

"Sam is saying something about you being with him?" I told her.

"Yes, I was. We were together when it happened."

"He wants you to know that although you had to experience it, he would not have wanted to go any other way."

Millie looked up and stated, "It was the hardest thing I ever went through in my life."

Suddenly Sam flashed a beach before my eyes.

"Were you two at a beach location? Sam is showing me a beach for some reason," I said.

Millie's voice conveyed sorrow as she tried to be strong, saying, "Yes, we were in Hawaii last Christmas and Sam and I decided to take a walk on the beach."

I started to feel Sam giving me pressure on my hand.

"Sam is telling me that he loves to hold your hand."

Millie started to break down in sobs. "That is what we were doing when he passed away! We were holding hands and he gripped my hand very hard just before he died!" she said through the tears.

It is not uncommon for me to feel a spirit at times grasping my hand to give the message to their loved ones that they still are holding their hands. But I did not know that this was Sam answering a question that had been plaguing Millie for some time.

"He knows this, Millie, but he's telling me that there was nothing you could have done for him, it was just his time to be in spirit."

With a look of relief, Millie said, "That is one of the questions I had for him. I wanted to know if there was anything I could have done. Was he hiding any signs from me?" she asked.

I quietly listened for Sam to respond to Millie's question.

"Sam is saying this with a smile and wants you to know that he had no signs and that he too was just as surprised as you were!" I told Millie this with the same levity Sam used when he told me.

This made Millie grin. "I guess we were both very surprised that morning then."

As the reading went on, Millie's mood started to lighten up as she was conversing with her husband. This is one of the best parts of a reading for me, when during a reading a person realizes that their loved ones who have passed are not gone and in fact continue to be a huge part of their lives. This can turn the reading from "are they with me?" into "what do they do alongside me every day?"

Millie had now relaxed and seemed to be enjoying this conversation with Sam, and excited about something she had recently done for him …

"Sam keeps saying the word 'art' to me, Millie; are you into buying or do you create art?" I asked.

"Not really," she replied. "No more than the average person, I guess."

"Hmm. Well, I know what I am hearing and Sam wants me to mention art for some reason. Did you just buy a painting?"

She thought about it and answered, "No, no painting."

I was certain of what I was hearing from Sam, but I thought perhaps he was not getting his whole message about this through to me.

"Okay, give me a second, I am asking Sam what he is talking about then."

I took a moment and asked Sam to reveal the specific art to which he was referring.

"Millie, for some reason, Sam is now laughing and talking about something you did for him." After I told Millie this, I took another moment in hopes that Sam was going to be able to get through to me what he was talking about, when all of a sudden, Sam flashed a tattoo to me.

"Millie, I know this may sound crazy, but were you thinking about getting a tattoo for Sam?"

Hearing that, Millie was beaming as she sat up in the chair and began rolling up her shirt sleeve. I thought to myself, this should be interesting…

Millie revealed to me a tattoo that was on her shoulder, it was a small airplane with the letters SRM underneath the plane, Sam's initials.

"WOW!" I said. "You got a tattoo! Now that is pretty cool!"
She smiled.

And with that I also was able to receive Sam's response as well.

"Sam is shaking his head at you with the biggest smile on his face!" I told Millie. "He says that he cannot believe you, of all people, got a tattoo in memory of him!"

"I never in my life thought I would! Millie replied. "I never much cared for them when I saw them on people, but a few months ago, I asked Sam to give me a message. I was going through the channels and came across a show that was showing people with tattoos. The one story I watched was of a person who decided to get a tattoo dedicated to a loved one who had died and my friend jokingly suggested that I should do the same. All of a sudden, I heard Sam whisper in my ear, DO IT! So I thought, why not, I'm a free spirit, I'll do it. So my friend and I looked up the location of a tattoo parlor and decided to go. I was nervous and made her come with me. I didn't know which tattoo I was going to get but I hoped that Sam would give me some sign once I arrived. As we drove to the shop, I didn't realize until we got there that it was near the airport, and bingo, I knew this too was another sign from Sam. So, on my arm, I decided to get a small tattoo of an airplane, the place where Sam and I first met!"

I could feel the pride and happiness emanating from Sam and I relayed this to his loving wife. While I was doing so, Sam lifted up his shirt sleeve and showed me the same tattoo on his arm.

"Millie, guess what? Sam is showing me that he too got a tattoo…just like yours!" I exclaimed.

"Really? I was wondering if something like that was even possible," Millie responded, excitedly. "As I was getting my tattoo, I could feel Sam with me and told him that if I was going to do this for him, he'd better be doing the same!"

I laughed and could also hear Sam laughing.

"Sam says that it's possible for a spirit to get a tattoo as well, though it was a little different for him, he says," I replied.

"Oh, how is that?" asked Millie.

"Let's just say it was a little less painful than it was for you," I told Millie.

"I'll bet it was!" she replied.

"And Sam is telling me that he refers to your tattoo as 'ink art' and says that you can refer to his tattoo as ink art as well."

Millie smiled with tears in her eyes. "I will. I will do just that," she said as she clapped her hands together. "I will tell people when I show them that it is my ink art, and it is dedicated to the one I love."

I replied, "And Sam promises he will do the same!"

———

Millie was grateful for the messages she received from her beloved Sam and was thrilled that Sam was happy with her new "ink art" on her arm. As I was getting a closer look at her tattoo, she told me that every time she looks at it, it takes her back *to when she and Sam were together. As she was saying this to me, a single tear rolled down her cheek. I told Millie that she had been so blessed to have been and still continues to be in a relationship with someone who loved her as much as she loved him. I told her that the tattoo was a great way to commemorate a special time or a special someone and that she should be happy each and every time she looked at her tattoo.*

11. NEVER FORGETTING

———

It was hard for Ted to remember any negative times he had spent with his loving wife Grace. It was also hard for Ted to remember all of the wonderful times he had spent with Grace as well. In fact, it was hard for Ted to remember any of the forty-plus years he had spent with his loving wife Grace.

Ted had Alzheimer's and had been living his last years with Grace having no memory of her, his family, and his life at all.

———

As the years had started to fade from Ted's mind, Grace would speak often about their past and relive the beginning days of their relationship.

In his younger days, Ted loved to hang out at the beach. Hailing from Florida, with the beach almost in his back yard, he would spend his days hanging out with his pals and of course trying to pick up girls. As a teen, Ted was always stick-thin and his buddies gave him the nickname, "Slim." Ted would laugh when he was called this because even though he was not particularly muscular, nor tall, and having what he thought were average looks, somehow Ted always got the girl. His friends never understood why this was, but Ted had something the others did not, a great sense of humor.

Ted had always made people laugh as a child and as a teen. He knew just how to use it on any girl he was interested in. This is how he won Grace's heart.

Grace had met Ted back in the sixties. Grace and her family had just moved to Florida. She made friends quickly, with her warm personality and dimpled smile. One bright sunny summer day she decided to go out with some of her friends to the nearby beach. Ted was a lifeguard at this beach and Grace, along with her friends, had set down their towels and belongings in a spot near the lifeguard stand where Ted was stationed. Always attentive, Ted noticed the girls near him and though he kept a steady eye on those in the water, he could not help but notice this group of girls sitting next to him. He could hear the girls laughing and giggling and would see them pointing at him from time to time. He could not imagine what they thought was so humorous about him and when his shift was finally over, he climbed down the ladder, walked over to the girls and asked them why they had been laughing and pointing at him. Grace, being the brave one of the group, stood up and told Ted that while he was sitting there, a young kid had come up behind Ted and was imitating Ted's every move.

Ted then turned around and saw the kid who was laughing at him as well and pretended that he was going to go after him. The kid started running down the beach and Ted turned back to Grace and started laughing. Ted was instantly struck by Grace's beauty and those adorable dimples that appeared when she laughed. Ted, thinking nothing ventured, nothing gained, took a deep breath and asked Grace if she would like to go out with him that evening. She looked at the other girls who smiled at her, then at Ted, and accepted his invitation.

That evening as the sunset kissed the sand with touches of pink, orange and yellow, Ted took Grace on a grand tour of his beach, as he liked to call it, showing her his favorite hangouts and telling her the places she and her friends should visit… when she was not with him, of course. The two of them laughed the night away as they shared their stories, holding each other's hands in the twilight.

From that night on, the two became inseparable and after a few years of dating, they decided to get married. The wedding of course took place around the lifeguard stand where the two first met.

As time went by, the loving couple had grown their family by having five children: three boys and two girls. Ted's job as a contractor eventually took him and his family away from the beach they loved, but they would often go back to Ted's beach on vacation, and eventually bought a summer home close by where the family would spend as much time as possible there as their children also grew up and had families of their own.

It wasn't long after Ted's seventy-second birthday that Grace started to notice Ted's memory loss. He would sometimes fumble for their children's names, brushing it off as having too many kids, but as time went by, Ted would even forget major events, coupled with a loss of time. Ted would make a joke about it, stating he'd better slow down on his drinking, even though he never drank much. So at Grace's insistence, she and Ted went to see his doctor, where he was diagnosed as having early stage Alzheimer's. When the doctor told them both the news, Ted turned to Grace and jokingly asked her if the doctor was ever going to take their food order. She slapped him on the shoulder and told him to behave himself as a tear started to run down her cheek. Ted wiped it away and smiled, reassuring her that everything was going to be okay, as he had always done in the past.

As the years went by, Ted's condition became increasingly worse, until he was unable to leave his home. It was at this time that Grace decided she and Ted would live out his remaining days at the place they first met, Ted's beach.

In his last months, all memory of his loving wife Grace and his family was erased from Ted's mind. Grace would still tell Ted about their life together and how he made her laugh, but none of what Grace was telling Ted made any sense. She and his family were now complete strangers to him and he could not comprehend who they were, or where he was, any longer.

Although Ted passed away with what in his mind were strangers with him, in fact his loving children were by his side, along with that girl he met on his beach and fell in love with…just a few short blocks down the road.

———

I spoke with Grace by phone and asked her who she wanted me to make a connection with, and she told me she wanted to connect with her husband Ted.

———

I began. "I have your husband here and I can tell that he has a great sense of humor as he is laughing and wants you to know that he's been hanging out at the beach."

Grace replied with excitement, "That's where we lived!"

"Oh! I thought this was just something funny he was trying to get across, as if he has been on vacation, but it's actually a confirmation for you two!" I exclaimed with a laugh.

"Oh no, that was something I was hoping he was going to bring up," said Grace.

"Well, he tells me that you always told him he never listens, but see, he heard you!" I replied. "Ted also wants you to know

that even in spirit, he not only hears you, but sees you as well as your family every day!"

"I feel him with me," Grace replied, happily.

"He says you should, because he is your guardian angel. But he stresses the word 'guard' for some reason?"

"Ted was a lifeguard when we met!" she answered excitedly.

"He's saying he will always take care of his girl!" I relayed to her.

I could hear Grace sniffling over the phone at hearing Ted's last comment.

"Speaking of caring, Ted is telling me he is excited that it is his turn again. He knows how much you did for him and wants you to know how much love he has for you for doing so," I told her.

"There was never a question that I was going to take care of my husband," Grace replied with conviction.

At that moment, Ted started to give me a strange feeling in my head. I will ask the spirit I am communicating with to give me a feeling in my body that correlates to how they passed as a confirmation. But since the sensation I was feeling was not painful, I knew Ted was telling me that it was a slower passing.

"Did Ted pass with some type of brain trauma?" I asked.

"He had Alzheimer's," Grace replied, her voice quivering.

Ted responded with a joke. "Ted is telling me he forgot that he had it."

Ted's response made us all laugh.

Happy again, Grace quipped, "Tell Ted to behave himself!"

"He wants you to know that those words are music to his ears," I replied.

"And his are to mine," Grace added with love.

"Your husband wants you to know how much he appreciated your staying with him during this challenging time. He is showing me other family members with you who also helped."

Grace responded, "Yes, our children were a great help, especially during Ted's last days."

"Last days? Ted says it sounds like he died or something," I told Grace.

We again all laughed at Ted's remarks.

"Ted wants you to know that there is no such thing as one's last days. He is telling me that, now being in spirit, he not only has all his memories back, but wants you to know that he will continue to make new ones with you as well!"

"I am counting on that," answered Grace.

"Ted is bringing up something about a house. Did you just move?"

"Well, sort of. I decided to move into our summer home in Florida. We lived many of our years there and I wanted to be where I felt his presence the strongest!"

"Ted wants you to know that even though he is able to be anywhere with you, he is happy you decided to go back to the beach house as he knows how relaxed you will be there. And don't get him wrong, he will be relaxing right beside you. But *he is telling me something about your not relaxing for long. He is showing me a baby; you're not pregnant, are you?" I asked, laughing.*

"My goodness no!" Grace said, laughing as well.

I knew she wasn't but when a spirit shows me a baby, this usually will tell me that someone is expecting a child.

"Our youngest son and his wife are expecting their first child in a week and we are all thrilled about it!" she exclaimed.

"But Ted is showing me your son and his wife in your home. Do they live with you?" I asked.

"Yes. My son and his wife decided to also move to Florida and I told them they could stay with me for as long as they wanted."

"Ted is laughing and tells me to tell you to watch what you wish for."

"Well, he knows how happy I am that they're with me and I can't wait to take care of the new baby!"

"He says there is no better mother around!" I relayed to her.

"He also has a clue about the new arrival," I said.

"What's that?" she asked.

"The baby will have your smile!"

"Oh my gosh!" she cried. "He loved my dimples and told me that was why he married me!"

I responded, "Only one of many reasons, Ted says."

———

It can be difficult to watch someone with this disease slowly lose all the memories of a life once lived and shared. But the key to remember is that the memory loss is only temporary and only applies to this body, as the soul will continue to keep all of the past memories as well as making new ones, forever.

12. Spirit Crush

Keep in mind that even though your loved ones in spirit know a lot more than any of us can ever imagine, they are still who they always were, personality included.

When I communicate with those on the other side, I not only hear what they say, see what they wish to show me, but I also "feel" who they are, their personality. And with that, I am able to convey the messages in the way their loved ones knew and how this person would express themselves.

And of course with the different personalities I encounter with spirits I have communicated with, just as with people, there are those who can be quite memorable...

Kathy and I were traveling, doing an in-person event where we met a young woman named Rhonda, who wanted me to make a connection to her brother Jamie, a young man who passed away in an accident at the age of thirty-three.

Once we sat down and I made my connection with Jamie, I could instantly feel that he was full of personality, someone who had enjoyed life here as well as continuing to enjoy life in spirit. The first thing that Jamie wanted Rhonda to know was that even death could not mess up his good looks and that he was now getting compliments on them from angels. I thought that was an unusual way to start off and we all began laughing. Rhonda remarked that Jamie would always get compliments on his looks, though they would never go to his head, but he would always joke about his looks, just as he was doing now. It was a wonderful and hilarious confirmation for Rhonda.

As the reading continued, the subject about what Jamie was doing in Heaven came up and he started to talk about how of course he was still with Rhonda and her family, so happy that he was able to help guide them in this life when needed. And even though they were frustrating him by not always listening to him, he had all the time in world, and in Heaven. Rhonda thanked him for helping them in the ways that he could and even confirmed that she was in fact feeling his presence. I could understand why, as he had a vibrant personality and his love for her was strong.

———

As the reading went on and I was relaying messages from Jamie to Rhonda, Jamie told me to tell Kathy that he thought she was very attractive. I started grinning at what Jamie had just told me to do, but I just went with the flow and told Kathy that Jamie thought she was very attractive. Kathy looked a little surprised, smiled, and thanked Jamie.

As the reading continued, Jamie not only kept talking to Rhonda, but kept giving me other compliments to tell Kathy, such as how well she dressed, how he loved her eyes, and so on. So at one point I finally just said out loud to all that I thought Jamie was hitting on Kathy! We all laughed as Rhonda confirmed that she too thought that Jamie had a little crush on Kathy. Kathy, going along with it, asked Jamie to describe himself. Jamie told her that if you were to put Brad Pitt, William Levy, and a Greek god all together that would be him. Rhonda then pulled out a picture of her brother and you know what, he was right. He was that extremely good looking! Kathy told Jamie that his physical looks were just as attractive as his personality. Jamie then instructed me to turn to Kathy and continue to give her the remainder of the reading. When I did what he asked, we all laughed and Rhonda asked Jamie, what about her! Jamie told me to thank Rhonda for introducing Kathy to him, that he was in love with her and that he would speak to Rhonda another time. Again we all laughed, but I did continue to give the reading to Rhonda.

Toward the end, Jamie told Rhonda to assure the family that he would always be with them. Jamie then asked Kathy if it was okay if he could drop by every now and then just to say hi to her. Kathy obliged and asked Rhonda if she had an extra copy of his picture ... we all laughed.

PART THREE

❧

MOVING
FORWARD

One of the biggest mistakes people make is believing the assumption that moving forward means having to let go of the person you loved who is now in spirit. With the work that Patrick and I do, we have found that this is one of the greatest misconceptions we encounter when speaking with people whose family member or friend has passed into spirit.

Many times, a person's belief is that yes, their loved ones are in spirit, but there is a separation existing between the two.

In the following pages I have included some suggested activities that will help you to remember old memories as well as create new ones! These exercises will help you move forward in this life, along with your loved ones in spirit.

13. Continuing Lives with Spirit

––––––

When someone you are in love with passes into spirit, it seems as if time and life come to a complete halt. You may feel as if a piece of your soul has also died along with that person, and sometimes even your will to live.

But the truth of the matter is, your life continues and so does theirs.

––––––

When someone you love passes, a multitude of feelings may appear, some being...

- Heartache
- Sadness
- Loneliness

- Guilt
- Abandonment
- Anger

The reason these feelings are so strong is because when someone they love passes into spirit, most people may feel as if the love they were able to give to this person as well as receive back has now come to an end. Even if they believe in an afterlife, they may experience a disconnection with that person not being here in the physical world and may become convinced that the love connection they once shared with one another has ended.

Then there is the physical anguish of not being with the person any longer. From living together, working together, having a physical relationship, enjoying life together, to even taking care of one another, these activities take up your time, a time that is now not being filled.

In order to move forward, it is important to understand what that means and how to fill both the emotional and physical voids that one may be experiencing.

When a person passes into spirit, their soul will leave the body, which opens the door to what we call Heaven, but it does not close the door to *this* physical world. Though there is nothing wrong with reminiscing about the past, as this can bring up the wonderful memories and feelings you once shared with a loved one in spirit, (we will discuss this later in the book) it is important to know that your loved ones in spirit are more than just memories.

Spirits see and experience all that Heaven is, but they also continue to experience and partake in their loved one's life here as well. Remember that there is no separation between you and your loved one in spirit. Although you may not feel them or see them as you had done in the past, their perspective of you has not changed. Well, I guess it has changed as they not only continue to see you, hear you, and feel you, but they see and feel your soul as well. Remember that one of the happiest things they are able to experience being in spirit and in Heaven…is you!

By understanding that your loved ones in spirit not only continually exist with you, but are also helping to guide you in this life, you will learn that it is imperative for you to continue living to the fullest. This not only helps you, but helps your loved ones in spirit as well.

Three's Company

When the three-year anniversary of the passing of Jake's wife, Brooke, was approaching, he decided to do something different. Instead of just staying at home as he normally did in years past, he decided this time he would venture out and take that trip to California, somewhere he and Brooke had always wanted to go but never seemed to find the time to do so.

When he was younger, Jake worked as a reporter for his hometown newspaper. As it was a small setup, Jake would do the reporting, take the photographs, and would even sell ads when necessary. He loved his job, as his hometown meant so much to him. All of his life he dreamed of being a big-time reporter in a large city. When he was young, he would interview his family and friends and then write stories about them and post them on the fridge. As he got older he developed a love for photography. He studied broadcasting at school and during the summers he interned at a major magazine in Washington, DC. Close to graduation time, he realized that he missed his hometown and didn't want to move to a big city. He came home and got a job doing just about everything at his local newspaper. One day his editor gave him the assignment of photographing and writing a short story on the community dance recital that was to be held in two weeks. He was to visit the dance studio and come up with an angle for a piece that would run in Friday's edition. The recital had taken out a big ad in the paper that day and the article would run in that edition. Not too happy with the assignment, he begrudgingly went off with camera in hand.

Once at the studio he made his way through all the little girls giggling and trying to pay attention to the dance instructor. She was a woman in her sixties and brandished a cane that she would pound hard on the floor if the kids did not pay attention. This was going to be a challenge. Looking around for a photo location, he noticed a smaller room toward the back of the building. The door was open and he could hear someone singing. He peeked inside to see a beautiful young girl holding hands with a young child smiling and swaying to the song she was singing. The young girl was dressed in a pink dress with *sparking sequined shoes on her feet. Why were these two alone in this room? He wondered. When he approached the two they seemed surprised to see him there. The young lady smiled and assured the child that it was all right. She introduced herself as Brooke and the child as Melanie. Jake introduced himself and explained why he was there. Brooke asked Melanie if she felt like joining the rest of the group and she nodded yes. Brooke then walked Melanie back to class and Jake followed. Brooke and Jake began talking, and she explained that Melanie and several other students had severe cases of autism. When they felt that the regular class was too demanding for them, she would pull them aside in a room and dance with them. There would be no pressure, no expectations, just a special time for them. Brooke explained that her mother was the dance teacher he had seen in the main room. Her mother had a younger sister with Down syndrome who was quite introverted. Being a dance instructor most of her adult life, she would teach her sister to dance in order to make her feel like a regular kid, and special. It worked, and her baby sister became more extroverted and enjoyed her life. Word got around and the dance studio was known throughout several counties for specializing in helping kids with disabilities.*

Jake was impressed by how warm and kind Brooke was. She was so gentle with the kids and talked lovingly about each of them. Jake now had his story. He photographed and interviewed Brooke and her mom, thanked them, and was about to leave. As he was heading out the door, Brooke asked him,

"*Didn't you forget something?*" *No, he thought, as he turned back, and Brooke told him he forgot to ask her out for coffee. He was not only taken aback by her kindness and beauty, but her boldness as well. He loved it. They went out for coffee and never looked back.*

Jake and Brooke had been married for six wonderful years before Brooke passed suddenly and without warning of a brain aneurysm. Jake took her passing hard, and stopped going out socially with his friends, something that he and Brooke used to do often.

But this year, Jake had a gut instinct that instead of just sitting around the house all day thinking about the wife he loved and missed so much, he would get away from this self-torment and finally take that trip to California. If nothing else, it would do him good to embark on an adventure.

Standing at the edge of the Pacific Ocean, Jake took a breath of the fresh air, mentally and physically revived. He watched the sun slowly make its way down over the distant horizon while gulls flew overhead as if they also were enjoying the beauty of this magnificent sunset. The sky was aglow with oranges, pinks, and yellows. It was an amazing view as the setting sun changed the colors of this natural canvas. While sitting on the beach and absorbing the sights and sounds around him, Jake watched couples walk up and down the beach, noticing one young woman who was taking pictures of the ocean as the sun's last rays reflected off the water. Jake was thinking that Brooke would have loved being with him here and at one point, he thought he even felt her there with him. But of course Jake just chalked that up to wishful thinking, as he would always do when that feeling came over him.

As the daylight vanished into the dusk of night, Jake stood up, brushed the sand off his clothes and headed back to his car. When standing at his car, he noticed the young woman who had been taking pictures on the beach seemed to be having trouble with her car a few parking spots over. Jake decided to go over to see if there was anything he could help her with and as he approached, he noticed that the trouble she was having was a flat tire. Jake introduced himself and asked if he could give her a hand at changing the tire. She told Jake that her name was Katheryn and she would be grateful if he could help.

As Jake began changing the tire, the two started talking about themselves, photography, and the sunset they had just witnessed. When Jake mentioned that he was from Tennessee, Katheryn told Jake that she too was from Tennessee and that she had moved to California a few years back for a job opportunity. When Jake asked her if she liked living in California, she told him that she did, although it was a much different world. If the opportunity ever arose for her to move back, she would consider it, as she missed her home state and being close to her family and old friends.

As Jake finished changing the tire, he told Katheryn that he enjoyed talking with her and asked her if she would like to meet there the next day to continue the conversation. She told Jake that she would love that. So Jake and Katheryn did meet the next day and the day after that until it was time for Jake to leave the state to return home. Katheryn drove Jake to the airport and told Jake that she would be coming to Tennessee in a few months, and would love to see him when she was there. This brought a smile to his face and he told her that she could bet on it.

Between phone calls and texts, the two kept in touch, and a relationship started to develop. When Katheryn did get to Tennessee, she and Jake made arrangements to meet and they were able to spend more time together, and that was when they both knew they were starting to have strong feelings for one another.

Jake was happy about his new budding romance, but underneath it all he felt a little guilty at the same time. He loved and missed his wife Brooke, but he could not ignore the fact that he also was starting to feel something for Katheryn. He knew in his head that Brooke would want him to be happy, but the love that he had for her almost made him feel as if he had been cheating on her.

Jake came to see me hoping to get a message that would help ease his guilt.

———

"Jake, Brooke is starting off by telling me that her passing was painless and quick."

Jake replied, with tears in his eyes, "Very."

"I'm feeling tension in my head. Was this some sort of brain aneurism or head injury?" I asked.

"*That's exactly what it was, an aneurism,*" Jake confirmed.

"*Brooke wants you to know that there was nothing you could have done for her. It was just her time to be in spirit.*"

"*I can't help feeling guilty!*" Jake announced abruptly.

"*She is telling me to tell you to stop it. There was no sign of it coming and there was nothing you could have done. Again, she wants you to know it was her time.*"

"*That's hard to understand,*" he said, shaking his head.

"*Brooke says you have to trust her as you always have and wants you to recognize that God knows what he's doing.*"

Jake put his head down, began to sob, and said, "*She would always say that. God knows what he's doing.*"

"*Well, she still is saying it and she says she means it more now!*" *I said.* "*Because she knows him personally!*"

Jake lifted his head back up with a small smile, wiping the tears from his face. "*That's Brooke.*"

The reading continued and Brooke was able to bring through things about herself and both of their families, and the activities she had been watching them do.

"*Brooke is talking about you going to the beach,*" *I said.*

"*Yes, I did go on the anniversary of her death,*" *Jake affirmed.*

With that, Brooke gave me an image of the lower West Coast.

"*I understand this was in California?*"

"*How did you know that?*" *Jake asked, with astonishment in his voice.* "*It was Malibu.*"

"*Because Brooke told me and she wants you to know she was with you!*"

With tears starting to stream down his cheeks, Jake responded, "We had always planned to go there together, but never got around to it."

"*Well, she wants you to know you are wrong. Although it was not as you had planned, you both did go there together and she wants you to know that she enjoyed every moment there with you.*"

"*You know, I thought I did feel her sitting on the beach with me, but I thought I was just imagining it," he said, uncertainty in his voice.*

"*She is telling me you do that all that time with her," I relayed. "Brooke wants you to know that she works very hard at giving you these signs and she says that you piss her off when you just push them away as not being real. Her words, not mine. So you better stop it, she says!" I said with a smile.*

"*Okay, okay, I will!" Jake replied, smiling as well. "I used to always piss her off for one thing or another, so I see that it still happens." He chuckled. "I am just happy she was able to be there with me.*"

I could tell that Brooke was now also happy to see Jake's mood starting to lighten up, but I could also tell she had much more to say about the trip to the beach.

"*Jake, did you go to the beach alone?" I asked.*

"*I did," he told me.*

"*Hmm, that's funny, Brooke keeps showing me you with someone else, another female.*"

With that, Jake began tensing up as he seemed to know where this conversation was heading.

Jake replied, "I did meet this girl and…"

"And you fell in love with her." I completed Jake's sentence.

"Yes, I did. And I feel so guilty about it," Jake confessed.

"You don't need to feel guilty, Jake. Brooke wants you to know that she could not be any happier for you!"

"She couldn't?" he asked, with a puzzled look on his face.

"Brooke knows how much you love her and she loves you, and this will always be. But she wants to express how important it is for you to continue to be able to give your love to others as it will make you whole again," I conveyed to Jake.

"I do love Brooke so very much, and I never thought I would love someone ever again, or even want that. The feelings for Katheryn came out of nowhere and things just fell into place."

With that, I could feel Brooke get even more excited with the message she was about to give to her love, Jake.

"Brooke is saying to me, came out of nowhere? She says, who do you think helped arrange for you to meet in the first place?" I told him.

"It was Brooke?" he asked.

"Yes, it was! She says she had to pull some strings to make the timing just right for you and Katheryn to meet, and it wasn't easy!"

"Now that does make sense to me. When I think about it, there do seem to be a lot of coincidences that occurred for us to be together."

"Well, Brooke is saying you can just call her Ms. Coin-cidences!"

We all laughed with Brooke at her last statement.

"Brooke says she had to take charge on the day you two first met, and she had to take charge when you met Katheryn, too,"
I said.

"How does she feel about Katheryn?" Jake asked.

"She likes Katheryn very much, but again, she knew you would too!" I responded.

"Oh, that's right, if she helped me to meet her I guess she knew her before I did. How does that work?"

"She says don't ask!" I said, throwing my hands in the air, as I saw Brooke do the same.

Again we all laughed.

"Brooke wants you to know that it is important for you to continue to move forward with your life but remember that forward does not mean moving away from the love that you two share."

"That means the world to me," Jake responded softly. "That she still wants to be with me."

"She does and she will. She says she does not mind sharing you, as nothing could make her any happier than to see a smile back on your face," I replied.

Jake seemed relieved to have this burden lifted off his shoulders.

"So rest assured, Jake, Brooke will continue to be a part of your life. She wants you to know that she will continue to guide you and love you just as much as she always has."

"*Knowing she is still with me makes me so happy,*" Jake said, sitting up.

"*She says that someone has to keep an eye out on you, and by the way, don't worry, she knows when to leave a room, if you know what she means.*"

Jake looked confused and then a grin came across his face.

"*I was wondering about that!*" he confessed.

"*Wonder no more, she says when you are being intimate with Katheryn, she does have other things to do. There's something about a lifeguard in spirit she met while you both were in Malibu…*"

"*What?*" Jake shouted.

"*She's joking; at least I think she's joking because she is laughing,*" I told him.

Jake was happy to hear that Brooke was pleased—not only with his new relationship with Katheryn but that she in fact had a part in it. He now knew that Brooke was always going to be with him, loving him, and realized that his happiness would always make her happy.

14. Ways to Remember and Relive the Past

In life, one of the greatest gifts we have, or one of the greatest curses we have, depending on how you look at it, are memories.

Memories of a special relationship give someone the ability to reflect back on the past, remembering who they loved, and give them the chance to relive all of the wonderful times the two have shared. For most, seeing the sights and sounds in your mind and feeling all the emotions that you experienced during that time can instantly bring a smile to your face.

But for others, these memories that once placed a smile on their faces now bring about sadness, reminding them of a time that once was, but is no more.

This is where people can make the biggest mistake of their lives, not knowing that memories *continue* to be made with you and your loved one in spirit!

When someone you loved is now in spirit, although your perception is that the person is gone, their perception is quite different. The spirit of your loved one continues to live life with you, thereby continuing to make new memories with you every day! Everything you do each day, from everyday routines to adventures you may have, your loved one in spirit not only experiences these things right beside you, but they participate in them as well.

It is important to realize the following:

- There is no such thing as death.
- Your loved ones in spirit continue to be with you, always.
- Life is short and you too will be in spirit one day.
- You are never alone on this journey.

By knowing, not believing, but knowing all of the above and coming to the realization that you and your loved one in spirit continue to share this physical life, you can change the perception and outlook you have on life, turning any sorrow you may have when reliving those days back into the happy times they once were.

From now on when you soak in the moments you've had with a loved one in spirit, know that these are not the only or the last memories you will make with them, as each day you are creating new ones. Sure, it goes without saying, it is a lot easier to make memories if the person you love is still in the physical. But keep in mind, from their perspective, you are as physical as you ever were to them. This is just another benefit of being in spirit. And the more open you are to connecting with them and taking notice of the signs they will give of their presence, the more memories will be made!

———

The following are actions you can take in order to help recall some of those wonderful occasions you have shared with a loved one in spirit. These are activities you can do by yourself or with others, which will allow you to again relive all of those special times that are a part of you, and know that your loved one in spirit will also be doing the same alongside you…

Now you and your loved one in spirit go and make some new memories!

Love Letters

When two people are in a relationship, one of the most touching, heartfelt, and emotional actions a person can take is to put their feelings into words. From signing a card with love to writing out a full letter, love letters and notes will stand the test of time.

Some of you may have had the habit of writing your thoughts and feelings down for someone you loved who has passed into spirit, while others may not have ever even thought it possible or had the chance.

The good news is that it is never too late!

Your loved one in spirit can in fact still receive any message, note, or letter you write to them, which you can call, "Heaven's Special Delivery."

You may find it cathartic to express the love you have on paper for someone, as when you do, the physical act of writing may evoke deeper thoughts you may not have even known existed. So when you get a chance, take out some paper and a pen (okay, you can type it on your computer too) and write your loved one in spirit a love letter.

To be honest, your loved ones in spirit may cheat a little because more times than not, they will be standing right beside you as you are writing your feelings down, receiving them and loving you even more…

Memory Sparks

Don't you find at times you may be watching television or listening to the radio when suddenly what you are hearing or seeing brings up a memory of your loved one in spirit?

From a movie that you both watched together to a song you may had danced to, it is funny how these things can suddenly take you back to a special place in time that you shared with your love. This is called a *memory spark*. (Okay it is not an official term, but we thought it sounded good!)

When a memory spark happens, a person will usually feel one or two things:

- Happy to be reminded of the memory.
- Sad that it is only a memory.

This is why it is of the utmost importance to be in the moment when this occurs! Experience all the thoughts and feelings when this takes place, rejoice in the happiness, and push away any sadness that may bleed through. It will take practice, but enjoying these flashes of memories will enable your loved ones to experience the happiness with you!

Many sparks can take place during the day that will remind you of a loved one in spirit, not only music or movies. From working in the yard to tinkering with the engine of an old car, everyday experiences bring back thoughts of our lives with our loved ones.

It is critical not to think of these memories as activities you are no longer able to share with your loved one in spirit, as they will share these special times right along with you!

Once you change your perception about having these experiences, you will find that they can bring a smile to your face and lighten your heart.

It is a good idea not only to have these memory sparks by chance, but to take the initiative and make them happen. Take time to think about certain songs that enforced the strong connection between you and your loved one and actually listen to them purposely. You will find that by doing this, you may even *feel* your loved one in spirit with you, enjoying the time that you shared together and the time that you are *now* sharing together, making *new* memories.

Discovering Memories

It's always good to reflect back on your own personal thoughts and remembrances of your loved ones, but those may not be the only memories possible!

It is amazing how many different people's lives a person can affect while on this Earth and how many of these memories go unshared! How often have you gone to a gathering of friends or relatives and find you are bringing up past events you experienced with loved ones who have passed? More times than not, you will hear a story someone else shares of your loved one in spirit that you may not have ever heard.

This is why it is vital to make contact with those your loved one in spirit knew, and in this day and age, it could not be any easier! From emails, calling someone on the phone, to even paying them a visit, there are many ways to keep in touch with those who also have memories of your loved one in spirit, as the conversations you will have can bring back recollections of the long-forgotten past!

Reminiscing Walking

One of the easiest things a person can do to recall memories and to make a connection stronger with a loved one in spirit is simply take a walk!

When you walk, this can be a time of solitude when you are alone with your thoughts. Walking also raises your metabolism, which most of us think of as helping you to burn calories, which is true, but what also happens is that when your energy level rises, your ability to make a connection with your passed loved ones rises as well! This is why, when you walk, you may start to think about a loved one or a memory will pop up out of nowhere. The truth is that this is happening because you are sensing them there with you without even knowing it.

So no excuses, people! Take a little time out of your day and go for a walk (or treadmill, if indoors) and you will be surprised by the strengthened bond that may take place!

Place Memory

For many, just the sight of a particular place can stir up long-forgotten memories.

When a person visits a location that they have not seen in a long time, they will start to remember things from the past that took place there. Some will call it seeing ghosts from the past. Not actual ghosts (though that can happen too), but just visions in the mind's eye. It is almost as if, when you are standing there, you can actually see the past taking place, hearing the sound of voices and visualizing the occurrences as you relive these moments.

And going to such places can help bring to life those good times again.

Let's say you have not been in grade school for a few decades and you go back to attend a teacher-parent conference with your little one. Once inside the classroom, doesn't it feel like only yesterday that you were sitting in those tiny desks making new friends and fearing homework? The decades that have passed melt in your mind's memory and you're eight years old again. That's what place memory can do, dissolve the years between now and those experiences, and bring you right back to the event that took place.

So go to those places you shared with your loved one in the past and reflect back on the special memories, watching how it can all come alive!

Grave Mistake

One of the most common ways a person will reflect back on the past is by going to the gravesite of a loved one.

When visiting a grave, a person will usually think or speak out loud to the one who is buried there and reflect back, smiling at the happy times, crying at, or even apologizing for, the bad times. Many will even speak to the person in the grave about things that have taken place since their last visit.

And once a person leaves the cemetery, many feel extreme sadness as if leaving their loved one behind.

This is another misunderstanding.

It is true that your loved one in spirit will be at the gravesite, but it is not because they were there when you came and will be there when you leave, it is because they *came* with you and they will *leave* with you as you return home.

Your loved one in spirit will hear all that you have to say to them, as they lovingly stand beside you, listening to you and feeling all the emotions you have for them.

When this comes up in a reading given by Patrick, many times a spirit will actually fuss at the person getting the reading because when visiting the cemetery, that loved one will look down at the ground, speaking to the grave, when in actuality, the spirit is standing right next to them!

Remember, when speaking to a loved one in spirit, you don't have to be at the burial ground, as they can be anywhere you are.

When you reflect, think, or speak to your loved ones in spirit, they will be with you, and what you're communicating is of the uttermost importance to them! You can't make them any happier than by keeping the lines of communication open with them, because even if you don't realize it, they are doing the same with you, always.

Although going to the cemetery is an expression of love and a way of honoring your loved one, never feel as if you need to go to the gravesite of a loved one in spirit in order to communicate with them, as this can be done anywhere.

Modern Memorial

Living in the age of instant contact, we have the ability to communicate with one another wherever we are by the touch of a button.

Social media continues to become more and more popular, not just for the living, but for the dead as well! Now this does not mean that your loved ones in spirit are using Facebook or Twitter, as their communication abilities go far beyond what we could ever imagine, but these tools we have are also a great way to make a memorial to someone you love!

Also, a number of funeral venues allow you to place a page about a loved one in spirit on their sites in order to share all of your pictures and memories of this person. You may even be surprised by how many other people may join in with photos you never knew existed as well as share their memories about that loved one in spirit!

———

So when remembering the past, never look at it as what you don't have any longer, look at it as what you once enjoyed, what you can still enjoy, and what you will enjoy again one day.

15. Choosing Your Path and Stepping Forward

———

After a loved one passes, there can be many variations on how one might live their life after this loss.

- Some people will just stagnate, only living in the past with the memories of what they once shared with their love. They push the future away and refuse to think of the possible happiness waiting for them. Many of these people are angry and in a depressed state, not thinking about what they were fortunate enough to have, but only what they do not have any longer, not willing to continue moving forward in their lives.

- Some will choose to be happy with the memories they made with their love, cherishing what they once had, and even though they continue to enjoy life, they are content with the love they had but are not interested in seeking another.

- And others will be happy with what they shared with a past love, but are open to perhaps finding new love in the future.

These are a few examples of what people may feel after the passing of a loved one. The only negative choice is if a person tries to only live in the past and is not willing to embrace what awaits them. It is wonderful to think of the past, but a person needs to live for today and tomorrow as this is what being here is all about.

Holding On

Kevin and Carmen were two extremely attractive people. Kevin was a very handsome man who stood six feet, three inches tall. Being an iron worker gave him a physique that would make any bodybuilder envious. Carmen was a very beautiful woman with long brunette hair and green eyes. She felt guilty at times that she spent as much time on her appearance as she did, but with the compliments she received, it paid off. Besides being good looking on the outside, both had warm and generous souls.

Kevin and Carmen met in their early thirties and were attracted to each other right away. Carmen had a routine of going out on Friday nights with some of the girls from work. They would usually go to dinner and then hit the clubs. They had a favorite spot where they would go to end the evening, a little neighborhood bar around the corner from the club. It's where the girls could unwind and talk about the guys they met and danced with. Carmen and her friends walked into the bar as usual around 12:00 a.m. for a nightcap and as she pushed the door open a man was pushing it from inside. As he was much stronger than she was, it jolted her and pushed her backward. She fell to the ground as her friends gasped. The man who was trying to come out opened the door all the way, picked her up and let her lean into his shoulder. He held her there for a moment. She gathered her wits as he asked her if she was all right. They both stared into the other's eyes and the girlfriends had to say something to break the two apart. Kevin apologized as he wasn't watching where he was going and told them he wanted to buy them all a drink to make up for it. They agreed and sat at the corner table.

Carmen and Kevin talked until the bar closed and her friends excused themselves to go home. Kevin invited Carmen back to his place and she accepted his invitation. The two became even more acquainted with each other that evening.

As the days went by, any time Carmen was with Kevin, she felt as if no other man existed and the bond they shared emotionally and physically was like no other. Both had had relationships before but nothing like this one. It was as if they completed each other. They were attracted to each other physically but when they made love it was as if their souls were on fire.

After only weeks of being together, Kevin decided to take Carmen on a trip to the Bahamas. He knew that this was a place she wanted to visit and thought this would be a perfect setting for romance. He had never done anything as extravagant as this before but there was something special about this girl.

Getting to their destination was quite an ordeal. After flying into Miami and then taking a small plane to the Bahamas, they needed to board another, tinier plane that looked as though it was a leftover from World War II to bring them to their remote location and the hotel. The two locked eyes with each other during the bumpy last flight and held hands tightly and laughed. They wondered—what were they getting themselves into?

When the plane finally touched down on the rough landing strip, they breathed a sigh of relief. As Carmen embarked, Kevin swooped her up into his strong arms. The breeze from the ocean cooled them as they gazed at each other tenderly. A taxi picked them up and they made their way to the hotel. As the two went inside the hotel room, the large windows were open and the breeze from the ocean was blowing the sheer white curtains. The two turned toward each other and held each another in their arms. Smiling, they collapsed on top of the fluffy white comforter and gazed into each other's eyes, knowing they were in for the time of their lives.

———

After a few days of relaxation, both Kevin and Carmen de-cided to take a sightseeing trip on the island. They rented bikes and proceeded to venture off on a day of exploration and dis-covery. Little did they know it would be their last day together.

Carmen, wearing a turquoise-blue bikini, and Kevin, just some board shorts, rented a couple of bikes and started off on their adventure. As they traveled down trails on the island, the scenery was magnificent. But at one point, after about an hour into their ride, the warmth of the sun became overwhelming and the two decided to take a rest in a secluded spot. As they were sitting there, Carmen started to give Kevin a massage and the feel of his sweaty shoulders made them both start to feel even hotter. Kevin took Carmen's hands in his, laid her down and made love to her.

As the sun started to set, the two got back on their bikes to race back to the hotel. At one point on the trail, the road became narrow and Carmen rode in front of Kevin. After she went around a curve she looked back and saw that Kevin was no longer beside her. She turned her bike around and as she went back around the curve she was shocked by what she saw. Kevin lay motionless next to his bike. Carmen jumped off her bike and raced to Kevin, thinking that he must be unconscious from tak-ing a tumble, but when she got to him she found that it was much worse. Kevin was dead. As she cradled him in her arms, sobbing, paramedics rushed to the scene and the police were fi-nally able to get her to let Kevin go. Her heart and soul were crushed, and she was inconsolable.

————

After the autopsy report came in, Carmen learned that Kevin had a defective heart valve and this was what caused his passing.

Carmen was devastated. Even though she had only known Kevin for a few short weeks, her heart said that she had found her soul mate.

As the days, weeks, and months went by Carmen found it hard to get past the grief she had been experiencing since Kevin passed. Family and friends would try their best to occupy her time and even made suggestions that she should move forward in her life. Those around her could not understand why Carmen was so depressed. Though they knew she had feelings for Kevin, she had only known him for several weeks. Carmen understood why they would have that perception, but this was something that she could not explain, not even to herself. Although she was only with Kevin a short period of time, she felt as if she had lost the love of her life.

————

When I spoke with Carmen, it had been several years since Kevin's passing. Carmen had read my previous books and told me that she had waited before she had contacted me. Not that she was afraid of making a connection with Kevin, but she was afraid of what Kevin might have to tell her.

———————

"Kevin is making a connection with me now, Carmen, and I can tell right off the bat that he is a pretty big guy," I said.

Carmen replied, "He was a very attractive man, both physically as well as his personality."

"Kevin is smiling and thanks you for those kind words and says to tell you that you are still his beautiful gal, with the prettiest smile and warmest heart," I relayed.

"That means the world to me," Carmen answered, with a hint of a smile on her face.

"Wow," I said. "Kevin is letting me feel the love he has for you and it is extremely strong."

Carmen held her hands together tightly and tears welled up in her eyes.

"Kevin is adamantly telling me that you two are soul mates, do you understand that, and what it means?"

"I thought with all my heart that we were," Carmen said, as she began to cry. "I just didn't know if he felt the same way."

"He wants you to know that he did and still does! Kevin says that you two were and still are a perfect couple," I told her.

Carmen looked happy for an instant and then balled her fist up and pounded her other hand with it.

"I just don't understand why he had to die!" she said, shaking her head.

Feeling compassion for her, I said, "That can be difficult to understand, Carmen, but let me see what Kevin has to say."

I took a moment to let Kevin answer Carmen's questions. Although I know that there is always a reason for someone to pass into spirit, I will let the spirit use their own words to help their loved ones with that question.

"Kevin wants you to know that it was simply his time to be in spirit and is telling me that if he had to go, he could not have asked for it to be in a better place and with any other person."

With that, I asked Kevin if he could show me how he passed so that I might understand what he meant by what he had just said. In that moment, Kevin gave me the feeling of a natural passing, but at the same time, he kept showing me the sun. He also gave me the feeling of joy that he was experiencing during the time of his passing.

"Kevin is telling me that he was extremely happy during the time of his passing. He is showing me the sun, so I take it that he passed outside, but he also is telling me that he was not alone."

"That's right," Carmen said through tears. "Kevin and I were on a bike ride in the Bahamas when he had a fatal heart attack."

"Well, Kevin wants you to know that he could not have died a happier man . . . something about 'it's how every guy would want to die,'" I told her.

I could tell what Kevin was getting at, and I knew Carmen could too, although she continued to cry. What Kevin had just said put a small smile on her face.

"Kevin is also telling me that you did not know each other for long. Is that true?" I asked.

"It is. We only knew each other for a few weeks."

With that answer, I was taken aback by the connection the two shared. The degree of love that I was experiencing between them felt as if they had been together for a very long time. For two people to have experienced that intensity of love in such a short time was truly a gift for both.

"Carmen, I have to tell you that it is rare for me to make such a connection and feel such a strong love between two people that have not known each other for very long. You have been truly blessed by having such a relationship and you have to keep in mind that not only does he continue to love you, but he always will.

"Can I ask you something embarrassing?" she next said.

"Sure," I answered, wondering what her question could be. "Ask away."

"I feel, well, I feel that he—" With that she stopped and looked down.

"Don't be shy, Kevin says," I told her. "He is telling me that is not like his girl."

She smiled and stated, "Okay. I feel that he and I are, um, in bed together. I mean, really in bed together, some nights. Just like we used to be."

Carmen, along with me, awaited Kevin's response to that statement.

After a moment I told her, "Kevin wants you to know that he never left his baby. You two enjoyed each other heart, soul, and body, and that hasn't changed," I explained.

"Do you know the difference between just a thought and really feeling Kevin's presence?" I then asked her.

"Yes," she answered.

"Well, Kevin is telling me that you do more than just fantasize about him. His presence is really there with you, and you can feel him at times."

Carmen looked relieved to know that she had not been imagining this, but was still very frustrated.

"I am grateful for everything Kevin is doing for me, but I want more! I want to be with him!" she said, almost defiantly.

Kevin replied strongly. "The one thing Kevin wants you to do is to continue living your life. He is telling you this because he knows that you still miss him very much, but it is important for you not to want to be where he is. Do you understand what he is saying to you?" I questioned.

After a short pause, Carmen responded. "I understand. But why is it so wrong for me to want to be with him?"

"It is not wrong to feel that way, because of the love you have for him and your wish to be with him. But you have to understand that it is imperative that you continue living your life here because you have a purpose for being here. And part of that purpose is to let Kevin be a part of your life in spirit."

"I get what you are saying, but I just cannot get past Kevin."

"Maybe you need to redefine your definition of what getting past Kevin is. You love Kevin and you always will, as he does you. But you need to understand in your mind that being soul mates, you and Kevin will be connected always. Kevin wants you to know that it is okay for you to be open to new relationships, as it is important for you to continue to give out your love. And whether someone else comes along or not, Kevin wants you to know that your love for him and your connection with him will never be broken."

"I don't want another love."

"Kevin understands why you are saying this, but he also knows what could be up ahead for you, if you would allow it. He is telling me that you now know he is always going to be with you, even if you were to find another love. But remember that your happiness makes him happy."

"Okay, I understand. He just needs to help me to heal my broken heart."

"He wants you to know that he is doing that. He is saying something about having worked with metal and that your heart is stronger than any steel he ever laid his hands on. And once repaired, it will be as good as new."

This brought a smile to Carmen's face.

———

I spoke with Carmen another time and she told me that she had in fact met a new man in her life. And even though she still loved Kevin very much, she now realized that she could give her love to another as well.

Stepping Forward

To move forward after the passing of a loved one, you first need to release the grief you may be experiencing.

Try to think of grief as a wall, designed to protect and shield you from the initial emotional torment of losing someone. After a while, though, the wall of grief may not shelter you but can in fact imprison you. Grief can keep you from moving forward, and by doing so make it difficult for your loved ones in spirit to connect with you.

So moving forward with life means just that…moving forward with your life *along* with your beloved's life in the beyond. Keep in mind that everything you do can affect your loved one on the other side as well. But don't worry, they are there for the long run and will be with you every step of the way!

———

Here are several steps you can take to move forward in your life.

———

Change Your Mindset

When you live your life knowing, not just believing, that your loved ones in spirit continue to be a part of your life—this will change the way you live your life.

Having the knowledge that there really is no such thing as death, and that your beloved who has passed is actually safe, sound, alive, and still with you, will help you in developing the new relationship you can have with them. Once you start believing/knowing that your loved ones are and always will be a part of your life, you can start to enjoy the relationship you have with them in a whole new way. Of course, I recognize that this can be easier said than done. It takes work! But if you visualize in your mind that your loved one is right beside you and then notice all the signs and connections that they give you, you can continue the relationship anew.

Live Life

Living your life well and achieving happiness is the best action you can take for yourself as well as those in spirit. You are here in this physical realm for a reason, a purpose, and it is not only for you but for others as well. You have a gift that no other person in this world possesses and that gift is you being you. Although there are billions of people on this Earth, each is different. You have a reason to be here and it is up to you to discover what that reason is.

So to live life means you should engage with people, participate in activities, help others, do all the things that will pull you forward and give you the many waiting opportunities for self-discovery.

Continuing Your Connection

The final part to this new way of living that will help you to move forward is what is mentioned in the next chapter, and that is to continue your connection. When you are open and receive the signs from your beloved in spirit, this will give you the confidence and knowledge that come in acknowledging that they are with you always.

By understanding these concepts and taking these steps, you will find yourself letting go of the grief with new purpose in your life, one that is shared by you and your loved ones in spirit!

PART FOUR

RECONNECTING WITH OTHERS

The title of this section, reconnecting, may give you the impression that you and your loved ones in spirit haven't been connected.

This is not so.

The truth is that your loved ones in spirit have and will always be connected to you; it is you who may need to learn how to reconnect with them.

The following section will give you the understanding and tools to keep your connections alive with your loved ones in spirit.

16. Continuous Connections with Spirit

In order to reconnect with a loved one in spirit, you first need to understand why and how they are connected with you...

First, recognize that your loved ones who are now in spirit are still the same people that you knew and loved. Although their physical body has now changed and they are of course in perfect health, they are in fact still human beings, still have emotions, including the love they have for you! And it is because of this love and care for you that they are with you every single day, a part of your daily life.

Life doesn't end; death is just the transition to more life. All the positive and loving things we do here, we also will do on the other side. The act of caring for loved ones here in this physical world does not change when we transition, as it remains part of our very existence on the other side.

But the type of relationship you had with a spirit will determine how close they are with you and how they will help you in this journey.

I wish I could count how many times someone has come to a session with a heavy heart because they have been told to let go of their loved one—that they are holding them here and not letting them move on.

How crazy is that?

The answer is simple.

Your loved ones in spirit are with you always and we do not go on with our daily lives experiencing joy and happiness without connecting every day with those loved ones. We can thank goodness for that!

Keep in mind that there is no time limit for your loved one in spirit to be with you. One of the biggest misconceptions is that a loved one in spirit can only be with you for a certain amount of time before they have to make a transition to the next life.

Not so.

Once a person is in spirit, that transition is over . . . they are there. There is no in between, and actually, there is no here or there for a spirit. Those in spirit have the advantage of seeing that this world is actually a part of Heaven, and for spirits there is no separation between the two. This means there is no time limit for a spirit when with their loved ones here.

The connection starts the moment someone passes. Although they are experiencing a welcoming from family and friends on the other side, they are also with us, feeling our grief and loss. They are comforting us from that moment on with immense love and compassion. Keep in mind that the trials and tribulations we go through here give our loved ones in spirit the opportunity to help us grow from those experiences.

Usually, it is a person's parent, spouse, or child in spirit who will be the ones who will spend the most time with their loved ones here in this physical dimension. This is because the love bond is the strongest tie of all relationships. Just as in this life, these are the people who want to be and will continue to be a part of your life. And even though there may not have been a strong relationship with these people, in Heaven, a spirit is able to make up for lost time or missed opportunities.

———

Although it is usually the closest loved ones who spend the most time with you, there are other spirits who will want to drop by and pay you a visit as well.

These spirits are other family members such as grandparents, aunts, uncles, even friends who will come by to check up on you. But don't get me wrong, sometimes a person will have even a stronger relationship with these people than a spouse or romantic interest, and they will be the ones that will be the most present. At times when Patrick is giving a reading, a great-grandfather, aunt, or cousin will come through. The person receiving the reading will be quite surprised as they didn't have a relationship with them. The relative will know all about that person, though. They have been with them their entire life and have been watching over them. Often the person will say it makes sense, once it is revealed to them, as they had a sense of awareness about that loved one and felt close to them their whole lives, but didn't know why.

And there can also be times when a spirit you may not have ever known will come to help you. These spirits are often experts at a certain life experience you may be going through and know best how to help you in that situation. These spirits can also be known as "guides." They can range from artists helping artists or doctors helping with medical problems. These guides can be with someone for a short while, or longer, depending on the need.

———

Now you may be asking how long those you love the most are with you. Well, that depends.

Even though there is no specified amount of time a loved one in spirit will be with you, the time they do spend can be determined by what you are experiencing.

First, know that the ones you love in spirit will always be there in your time of need.

If you are going through tough times and have negative emotions such as grief, anger, or any form of pain, mentally or physically, your loved ones on the other side will be there, every time. Remember that they know everything you do and feel and want to help in any way they can during these times of trouble. This is what love is all about, even for those in spirit.

And how do spirits help you?

In many ways.

If a person is going through some physical challenge, such as an illness, those in spirit are able to help by making the connection with a person's energy and will assist in the healing process. But although there may be an illness that someone must endure such as an incurable disease, cancer, for example, a loved one in spirit will help to ease the pain as well as send comforting thoughts. Keep in mind that there is a reason for physical pain in this life as it gives that person experiencing it the chance to be aided by others here as well as in spirit, and this is what brings about enduring life lessons.

A spirit will also help their loved ones here emotionally.

If someone is going through grief, depression, or some other negative state, a spirit will spend a great deal of time with them in order to help them get through it. They can guide and comfort by suggesting thoughts and feelings, such as love, memories, and hope. It is these connections that can assist a person on the path to achieving a happier life.

But just as with anything else in life, even when the help comes from spirit, what they want to do with it is always up to the individual.

These are just a few examples of the countless ways a spirit will assist those they love. Their connection is not only just to help you, but to continue enjoying this life right alongside you as well!

A loved one in spirit is able to continue to experience all this world has to offer, still acting as your companion. They will be present as you do your everyday tasks, from going to work, enjoying the outdoors, to even watching television with you. That's right; spirits like to hang out at home too!

Another reason they like to hang out, in addition to loving you and your company, is that your mind is more at ease and you may notice their presence. And although there are many ways that you make a connection with a spirit, often it is unnoticed or denied.

Ghost

Linda awoke suddenly in the middle of the night, covered in sweat from a nightmare she had just experienced. She sat up in bed, patted her forehead with a tissue, and took a deep breath. Getting her bearings, she focused on the moon shining bright through her open window. Calming herself, and taking a sip of water, she tried to make sense of the disturbing dream.

Linda remembered that she was in a plane, seated next to her husband, Gary, as they were both coming home from a business trip. Suddenly they were shaken in heavy turbulence. Linda always disliked flying, but she especially hated to fly in small planes. During the turbulence, Gary grabbed her hand, held it tight, and told Linda not to worry, everything was just fine. With a hard jolt, the small engine plane shuddered and the lights went out. Linda felt her heart jump out of her body when she could feel the plane's nose start to dive, heading straight down and accelerating faster and faster toward the ground. She felt her body being pushed back against her seat and, grasping Gary's hand tightly, she looked at him and could not understand why he was smiling. Her head was spinning as the noise in the plane grew louder and louder. Lights flickered on and off and the buzz of the engine seemed to scream in her head. She knew this was it and before the plane was about to crash, Linda again looked at Gary and he just smiled, held her hand tightly, and said "I love you" to her. This is when Linda woke up with a scream.

This was not the first time Linda had experienced this disturbing dream, as it seemed to be an ongoing event. But this dream was different from the ones Linda used to have because what happened to her husband Gary on the plane was not actually a dream at all, it was reality. A year or so ago, when coming home from a business trip on a small plane, Gary's plane crashed due to an electrical storm and all onboard were killed.

Since the day of her husband's passing, Linda had felt extreme guilt for not being with him on the plane as she had been many times in the past. Her aunt had been ill and she'd wanted to stay with her and not accompany Gary on that trip. And even though she knew inside there was nothing she could have done, she couldn't help but think, maybe, just maybe.

After the dream, Linda got out of bed and went into the bathroom to splash cold water on her face. The water felt good and as she lifted her face up and looked into the mirror, she thought she saw a figure behind her. Though momentarily startled, she came to her senses, realizing that it was just a combination of the shower curtain and the cobwebs still in her head making her see things. So, feeling tired, Linda got back into bed and hoped for some undisturbed sleep.

Linda had kept active since Gary's passing. She wanted it that way. The busier she was, the less time there was to think about the would haves, should haves, and could haves of Gary's tragic passing. Linda had attended support groups in the past, but didn't feel comfortable sharing her feelings with other people, especially people she did not know. And although she could see that this group had helped many of its participants, she wasn't ready to share her story. It just wasn't the right time for her.

Christmastime was just around the corner, a time that had been extra special for both her and Gary. This was the time when the two had met. Linda worked at the makeup counter in one of the larger retail stores. It was a few days before Christmas and she was surrounded by ladies wanting to try the latest eye shadow and lipstick. As Linda was finishing up a makeover for a woman and began cleaning her station, she heard the next customer sit in the chair. And when Linda turned to help that person, she was surprised to see that the customer sitting there was a man! In fact, Linda was so startled she let out a little, "Oh my!"

There sat Gary, laughing, as he knew sitting there would give her a shock. Gary told her that a little eye shadow would be just fine. Linda was taken back at first. She then saw Gary look down at a little girl who had been watching the whole event. Gary indicated to Linda, with a gesture of his hand, that he wished for her to come close. He whispered to her that he was taking his niece Christmas shopping and she dared him to get a makeover. Now smiling, Linda winked and played along, telling Gary she had just the right shade for him.

After putting a little makeup on Gary, all three started to laugh and Linda told Gary how pretty he looked. Gary's niece agreed. Gary was impressed by how easygoing Linda was. So much so, Gary asked her out for coffee that afternoon as a reward for being such a good sport, and the two hit it off. And by Christmas the following year, Gary had proposed to her and she accepted. The two were married for three happy years, until the day the plane went down.

When Christmas came that following year, it was the first year that Gary was not going to be with Linda, and she decided it was not a time to celebrate, much less put up a tree. It would be just too painful. No Gary, no Christmas, and that was that.

Because of the grief she was experiencing, on many days Linda would not even go out of the house. She would fill her time cleaning her home, every nook and cranny, even if it did not need it. Just keep busy, she would tell herself, and she would vacuum up and down and wash this and that until everything was spotless, like it always was.

One day while vacuuming, Linda moved the couch over as she always had and noticed something shining behind it. When she bent down and picked it up, she recognized it instantly, a small golden Christmas ball with a hook. Linda got a little angry at herself for not seeing the ornament there the many other times she had vacuumed back in that area. But she figured that it must have been hooked to the bottom of the couch, and the vacuum had knocked it free.

When Linda came to me for a session, she told me that reading my books had helped ease the pain with Gary's passing. She said that although she believed in an afterlife, she hadn't received any signs from her beloved husband and wanted to know why. I told her that we would just have to see what Gary had to say about that.

Gary then made a connection with me. "Gary is giving me mixed emotions about his passing, Linda, but he's not talking about his feelings, but it's what you are feeling that concerns him. He is letting me feel a heavy guilty feeling; is this something you are experiencing, Linda?" I asked.

"Yes, I am," Linda replied, with her head down.

"He does not want you to feel this way any longer."

Gary started to give me an impression, and I asked Linda, "Did Gary pass by falling?"

"He died in a plane crash," Linda said. Tears began to well up in her eyes as she looked up.

"Oh, I'm so sorry to hear that," I said to her. "Gary wants you to know that there was no pain, none at all. And I can tell that he has a forceful personality and wants you to know that there was nothing you could have done. It was his time to be in spirit."

Linda took a tissue from her purse and began to weep.

"Linda, why would you think there was something you could have done to prevent his plane from crashing?" I asked.

Taking a breath, she answered, "I know it's not logical, it's just ... if I had been there, maybe we would have run late, or early, and maybe the plane would have missed the storm altogether."

I took a moment to hear Gary's response.

"Gary is asking the question, when were you or he ever late for anything?"

With that, a small smile came across Linda's face. "That's true," she said. "Gary and I are sticklers for punctuality."

I told her, "Gary says watch what you say about him to me or you are going to give him a bad reputation!"

"Oh my gosh! That is something Gary was always concerned about, his reputation! He said it was what set him apart from others in his field."

I smiled and responded, "I totally agree with him on that!"

Linda smiled too at hearing my statement.

I continued. "So please make sure from this day forward that you do not have those thoughts again, as this will make Gary very happy."

"Okay, I will. I mean, I won't. Oh, he knows what I mean," Linda responded, flustered.

Both Gary and I chuckled at Linda's response.

"Gary is bringing up the holidays, I know they are just around the corner, but there is something more special about them. Is there also an anniversary? He is holding up a cake and that is the symbol I recognize to indicate an anniversary," I said.

"Yes, it is when we met, and when he proposed. Not in the same year, a year later," Linda said, with renewed vigor.

"Gary is telling me that he would have married you that same year if you would have let him."

Linda shook her head and smiled. "Me too."

But as we were talking about the holidays, I became aware of a feeling of sorrow coming from Gary concerning Linda. Of course I knew Linda was going to be sad during the upcoming holidays, which was only natural. But there was something else Gary was saddened by.

"Gary knows how difficult this holiday season will be for you. He's saying something about your not even putting up a Christmas tree this year?"

"That is correct. I have no plans for doing so. I'm just not in the mood."

"He is telling me that he left you a sign to put you in the mood."

With that, I asked Gary to indicate further what he meant. Linda looked perplexed.

"Gary is showing me a couch, I'm not sure what he is referring to, but if a couch doesn't scream Christmas, I sure don't know what would!" I said, laughing, as I didn't understand what Gary was trying to get across to us.

Linda laughed at my joke, but then exclaimed, "I did just find a Christmas ornament behind the couch! There's no way he could have had anything to do with that…right?" Linda seemed puzzled.

"Gary says of course he did, who else?" I said.

"How is that possible?" Linda asked.

I could tell Gary was proud and I relayed, "He tells me you have been asking for signs… well, there's a pretty good one, he says."

"I just didn't think of a sign like that," she said, shaking her head.

"He says signs can come in many ways."

I could tell that Linda was getting excited now, know-ing that Gary had been trying to connect. Her spirits lifted.

"What other ways has he been letting me know that he is with me?"

I took a moment for Gary to answer her question.

"I know this may sound crazy, but Gary is showing me a bathroom, did you see or feel him there?"

"No, not that I recall…oh wait, there was one time when I had just woken up from a terrible nightmare. When I went into the bathroom and looked in the mirror, I thought I saw Gary standing there behind me!"

"And you passed it off as your imagination, right?" I asked.

"I did! I just thought I was still half asleep," Linda replied.

"Gary wants you to know he was standing behind you, trying to comfort you after your bad dream. But then again, he says he always has your back."

With that, Linda started to tear up and said, "He al-ways did."

Linda asked, "Can Gary tell me why I keep having the same awful nightmare? In it, I am with him on the plane when it starts to go down. It is a horrible thing; the plane is going straight down and I turn and look at Gary and he is smiling at me before it crashes. It is the same vision every time. Why?"

Hearing Linda's dream, I was anxious to hear what Gary's thoughts would be. And once I heard his answer, it all made sense.

"Gary says that this is not a dream, but it has been in fact a message from him that he has been trying to get through to you for some time. You have been wondering ever since the plane accident if he knew what was happening to him and if he was afraid."

"Yes, yes, that is one of my biggest fears; that Gary knew he was going to die."

I listened to Gary and then replied. "Gary knew from the way the plane was losing altitude and from the velocity that there was no way to survive such a crash, so there was only one thing to do. As it was going down, he closed his eyes and pictured the most important thing in his whole life, you. He says that he pictured you holding his hand and as you held it tightly, he kept telling you how much he loved you. This is why you see him smiling, he says. He wanted you to know that he was in fact smiling before the crash because he was thinking about you!"

What a wonderful message and what a strong and brave man Gary was. With that we both began to tear up.

It took a few moments for Linda to get past her emotional state in response to what Gary had just told her. She now understood what the dream meant, that it was not a nightmare, but a wonderful connection. It was Gary answering the question she had been struggling with for such a long time.

———

Linda finally was able to compose herself and stated, "That will stay with me forever."

"And so will he," I responded, repeating what Gary just told me to say.

Linda's face was flooded with relief and I could tell that a great weight had been taken off her shoulders.

"Gary is saying something about him being your Patrick Swayze like in the movie Ghost. He says you know what he means by that."

"I do! He knows that was one of my favorite movies and he used to always joke about us going to a pottery class together so we could reenact that famous scene from the movie," she said, excitedly.

"He says that he didn't realize that he was really going to be 'a ghost' by the time you two got a chance to do it!"

This made Linda burst into laughter.

"Tell him to stop joking about it," she said, grinning through her tears.

"He says that he is just begging you not to play 'Unchained Melody' if you do decide to start making clay pots," I told her.

Again this made Linda start laughing.

"He always hated that song," she replied.

"He wants you to know that although it's a great movie, the filmmakers got something wrong in it," I relayed.

"What was that?" Linda asked.

"He says that Patrick Swayze leaves Demi Moore to go to the other side and that is not the way it is. He wants you to *know that he can be there on the other side, and he can still be here as well and the one thing he promises is that he will always be by your side."*

Linda said through a teary smile, "I will count on that."

———

I spoke with Linda about a year later and she told me how much that first reading had changed her life. When she got home, she decided to put up a Christmas tree and decorate for the holidays for both of them. She said that she could even feel Gary holding her just as Patrick held Demi in the movie as she put the ornaments on the tree. She also placed the one she found behind the couch right on top so she could look at it and remember that it was their special ornament.

She also stated that since her reading, she never experienced the nightmare again, now understanding that all along that it had not been a nightmare, but a misinterpreted message from Gary.

Linda said that several times when she turned on the TV, the movie Ghost *was playing on one channel or another and she had even heard the song* Unchained Melody *on the radio. She knew these were signs from Gary and they brought a smile to her face every time.*

17. Common Sensing

———

One of the most common ways you make a connection with spirit is when you feel their presence.

Unfortunately, most people pass that off as imagination and dismiss what they are actually feeling, which is in fact a loved one's presence. This is unfortunate as, if a person is willing to accept that they are indeed sensing a loved one's spirit with them, this feeling or sensation that the spirit gives can gradually become stronger. Those who are open to receiving this connection and can feel their loved ones from time to time will find that this sensation usually lasts only a few seconds or minutes.

But one of the greatest misconceptions is that their loved ones in spirit are there with them only for these short periods of time.

This is not true.

It takes energy for your loved one in spirit to make their presence known and believe it or not, it takes energy from you as well. When that connection is made, the one in spirit can only sustain it for a short time, as they do not want it to affect you adversely, or them, and by this I mean draining your energy.

But remember, just because you may only feel them from time to time, this does not mean they are not with you. Your loved ones in spirit are constantly with you, as you are a principal part of their life, even in spirit.

If you want to make this connection with your loved ones in spirit, try this. While you are sitting down and relaxing, perhaps watching television or on the computer, close your eyes for a few moments and ask your loved one in spirit to let you experience their presence. Now if you do not understand what this would feel like, here is a tip. When you are in the same room with a person, close your eyes and have that person slowly approach you and stand there. Notice how the energy around you has changed and how you are able to make a connection with that person just by their standing there. This is exactly the same sensation that you will receive from a loved one in spirit. Again although it may be a slight impression at first, the more you tune into it, the stronger the sensation will become.

Another way to reconnect with a loved one in spirit is by asking them to manipulate something physical in your home, to give you what is also known as a "sign" from them. There are quite a few ways that they can do this and probably already have, but you are not connecting them with these occurrences.

It is common for a spirit to make sounds in a home. From taps, knocks, creaks to even footsteps, spirits have the ability to make these noises. Feel free to ask a loved one to do one thing one day and another, the next; you may be surprised at the response you receive!

Sometimes a spirit will have fun with you as well, and they will do this by moving or hiding an object. Ever put your glasses down on the table only to find them on the counter? How about your keys, that you know you put in the drawer only to find them on the dresser. Even though most of the time these pranks are just for the spirit's entertainment, as they watch you look for the item, sometimes an action is taken to actually help you. By delaying the activity you were about to participate in by your having to look for an item, they may have prevented some harm that you had been heading toward. Again, your loved ones in spirit are helping you in life.

Then there are those scents you may have noticed that remind you of your loved ones. Though this phenomenon can be harder for a spirit to enact, it can and does happen. We are not saying that Uncle Bob had smelly feet and you can smell them now, no. We're talking pleasant aromas or perfumes that will remind you of the person the moment you smell them. Our loved ones have the ability to manipulate the air around you, causing a certain scent to come through to you. So don't be surprised if you suddenly walk into the scent of a loved one that seemingly comes from nowhere.

The old wives' tale is that when a picture is hanging crooked on a wall, a spirit is present in your house. Sometimes this happens to be true. Spirits are able to make pictures off-balance to show you that they are present in your home. Go around your house and straighten any picture that looks crooked and check back in a day or two, you might be surprised by what you find!

Speaking of pictures, spirits can also appear in photographs. Although it would be wonderful to see a full figure of your loved one in spirit, what will usually appear is a light orb or a light smear, as this is what reflects off from your loved one's spirit.

Fifty Years

Jack and Christi met and fell in love at the ripe old age of seventeen. Jack worked at his father's garage and met Christi when she stopped in with her girlfriends to buy a soft drink.

It was a hot July afternoon and Jack would have rather been anywhere except working at the garage that day. All of his friends had either gone to the movies with their gals or to the pond. His father depended on extra help in the summer and Jack was it. Why not? Jack didn't have a girlfriend and always felt like a third wheel anyway. While Jack was changing oil

and fixing a flat in the garage, a car pulled up for gas. Jack's fa-
ther was on the phone and asked Jack to help them. Grumbling,
he wiped the sweat off his face and came to the gas pumps. There
he saw a red Chevy convertible. Jack thought, What a sweet
car, and then he got closer and could see it was filled with young
ladies. They all sat giggling with each other as the young man
approached the car, wiping the oil from his hands. Jack went to
the driver's side and the girl seated in the driver's seat told him
to fill it up. One of the girls asked Jack if he had a soda machine
and he pointed to the side of the building. At hearing that, they
all jumped out, all but one who was sitting in the back seat
looking through her purse, Christi. Christi was the prettiest gal
Jack had ever seen, but he didn't let on. She had brunette hair
and hazel eyes. He was mesmerized by her beauty and didn't
have the nerve to speak to her. Why should he? He thought she
wouldn't be interested in him anyway. It wasn't even his shop,
but his pop's, and she was out of his league.

The sun beat down on Jack as he pumped the gas. He couldn't
be happier that the pump took so long, as he didn't want Christi
to leave. Christi sat there silently, shyly looking at Jack, when
she quietly said she had better be joining the other girls. But as
Christi jumped out of the car, her purse caught on the door and
everything inside of it flew out to scatter on the ground. Jack
hurried over and bent down to help Christi pick up her items
and as he did, this most wonderful, most beautiful girl touched
his arm, thanking him for his kindness. That was all it took.
Jack mustered up enough courage to ask Christi if she would

like a soda pop; she accepted his offer and the two were never separated again.

After a few years of dating, Jack and Christi tied the knot and started their life as a happily married couple. Jack continued to work for his father and eventually took over the business. Christi was a stay-at-home wife although she would come in two days a week to help with the books. Together they raised four children.

As the children grew up and left the nest, Jack and Christi's love affair continued. Just as with any relationship, they had good times and not so good times; but the one constant was the love that Jack and Christi shared with each other. It got them through everything.

As old age started to set in, unfortunately Christi's health started to deteriorate. And after several tests and many trips to the doctor, the news Jack and Christi received was what no one wants to hear. Christi was diagnosed with cancer.

Of course, this came as a shock for both Christi and Jack, but even more shocking, Christi was given only a short time to live. Jack wanted to fight this thing to the finish but the doctors gave them no hope. All Jack could do was make Christi's last days the best they could be. They both agreed that Christi should stay at home, the place where she was the happiest.

The two would take walks together during the early stages of the illness and reminisce, recounting their life and many wonderful memories. When Christi couldn't take those walks anymore, she and Jack would sit on the swing on the front porch and talk for hours. When that became too much for her, he would sit by her bedside, never leaving the one he loved.

The few months that Christi had left seemed to fly by as if they were only a matter of days, and the days seemed to turn into minutes. Jack spent all his time nursing and taking care of Christi as she became more and more ill.

On her last day, as the morning sun was starting to rise, with its rays of light filtering in through the curtains on the bedroom window, Jack sat beside Christi as he had done every day since she had become bedridden, holding her hand and telling her how much he loved her. Barely conscious, Christi smiled as she looked into Jack's eyes, just like she did so many years ago at the garage, taking her final breath surrounded by her family.

After the children all left, Jack stayed in the room by himself for a while as the memories of the life he shared with his love came flooding into his mind. As Jack looked down at Christi, he did not see the frail woman lying there in bed; he saw the beautiful young girl he fell in love with all those many years ago. Jack bent over, caressing Christi's face gently, and gave her one last kiss with tears streaming down his face, whispering softly to her that he would love her forever.

Several months had passed when Jack came to see me at one of the in-person events that Kathy and I do, and scheduled a meeting with us.

"Hi, Patrick, I am so happy that you were able to fit me in on your travels," Jack said, as he seated himself in front of us the next morning at our private session.

I shook his hand he said, "My pleasure, Jack. I am happy that time made a way for me to be able to do this today."

"I am very grateful about that, too," Jack replied. "I was at your live show last night, but was not one of the fortunate ones who got a reading, and was happy to hear from your assistant that you had time to give a few personal readings today," he said, sitting up in his chair. "I booked you as fast as I could before anyone else could grab the spot."

"Well then, since you were at last night's event, I won't go into details on how I work; I'm sure you heard it all last night," I said.

"I did, and I thought you and Kathy were just wonderful." Jack said.

I replied, "That is very kind of you to say. So, Jack, who is it that you would like me to connect with today?"

"My departed dear wife, Christi," he answered, with sadness in his eyes.

"Okay, Jack, give me a moment and let me see if I can contact her."

I took a moment to open up to spirit. It took no more than a brief moment before Christi was ready to speak.

"Christi is here, Jack, and I can tell you she is starting out by letting you know how much she loves you."

When I connect with spirit, it is not unusual for me to feel the emotions of the departed for the loved one for whom I am making a connection, and love is certainly not uncommon. I will usually tell the spirit that I will relay their feelings further

into the reading, but if they push the feeling extra hard on me,
I know this is the first thing they want their loved ones to hear
from them.

"Christi is showing me that she is able to stand up again,
to move," I told Jack.

"Oh, I was so hoping she would be mobile again. She so
hated being bedridden and I had to take care of her for so long.
I never minded, though; she was my sweetheart, and I would
do anything for her."

"She shows me she was at home when she passed into spirit,"
I said.

"Yes." Jack's eyes filled with tears.

"She says that even though it was difficult, it was a very
meaningful time," I replied. "Christi is telling me that she
wants you to know that even at the end, she knew you were
right there by her side."

Jack's tears continued. "I knew she did."

"She wants you to know that she still is your love and
that it is now her turn to take care of you."

"She always did," Jack replied.

"And always will!" I said. "She wants you to know that
you are soul mates and that the love you share will continue."

Jack sobbed.

I then said to Jack, "Christi is giving me the impression
that you two were always together."

"That's right. We were inseparable."

"*You also worked together, did you not? She is showing me this.*"

"*Yes, I have a garage, or rather, I had one. It is my son's garage now. She and I worked there until the day she became ill. She was the smart one, and always took care of the books.*"

"*But she is also saying something about your father, was he a part of that too?*"

"*Yes, it was his garage first and I worked there as a young man, and that's where I met Christi,*" Jack replied.

"*Christi is telling me she is with your father and he wants you to know that it was the luckiest day of your life when she came to the garage.*"

This put a smile on Jack's face.

I continued. "*Christi says that even a garage can be the most special place on Earth, when love resides there.*"

"*She is right on that. But again, she was right on everything,*" Jack said.

"*Christi is smiling and saying if only that was true.*"

"*She knows it is,*" Jack said, nodding his head in affirmation.

Christi continued the conversation by talking about their children and giving some advice on what paths they should think about taking. She even mentioned that she was aware of a new baby coming into the family and this brought a bigger smile to Jack's face as he told her that it was going to be a girl and would be named after her. I could tell that this made Christi proud.

Christi also indicated that one of her children was about to get married and asked Jack to let everyone there know that she wouldn't miss it for the world. Jack told her that he was saving her a seat, front row. And speaking of weddings, Christi then turned the conversation toward hers and Jack's own special day.

Jack looked down to hide his emotional response.

"Christi is telling me that you and she have a special anniversary coming up and is showing me an image of gold. Is it your fiftieth wedding anniversary she is speaking about?" I asked.

With that, Jack looked up at me as he tried to regain his composure. Tears started to stream down his cheeks.

"Yes," Jack replied with a quiver in his voice. "Our fiftieth wedding anniversary is coming up in a few weeks and we had always planned on celebrating it by taking a cruise. That was until Christi became sick. As Christi was lying in bed, we both knew that there was not going to be a cruise, but we kept planning the trip as if she was going to get well enough for us to take it. That was important, as we waited a lifetime for that celebration. Even though it has been fifty years, it seems like yesterday when we met for the first time. We never took time for ourselves and this was the trip where we would."

Hearing the way Jack described their plans made Kathy and I tear up as well.

I told him, "Jack, Christi wants you to know that during the time of her illness, even though you both knew deep inside that she was not going to make it to your special day, just talking about it with her and making those plans made it seem as if you were both on the ship together, both in perfect health and it was almost as if she could feel the ocean air on her face. She wants you to know how much that meant to her and helped her with the pain she was experiencing."

"Thank you, Christi, for saying that," Jack replied. "Believe me, Patrick, it helped me a great deal too."

I continued. "There is something that Christi wants you to understand. You both will make it to your fiftieth anniversary."

"What do you mean?" Jack asked, puzzled.

"Christi wants you to know that by her being in spirit, she is still with you, in perfect health, and is still with her sweetheart! She wants you to know, Jack that not only will she be with you on your special anniversary, but she will be with you each and every day, forever. So when each future anniversary comes, continue to add the candles on the cake for the years together, not stopping at the forty ninth one, as your life together goes on and your love does not end but continues always."

Jack smiled through the tears and seemed to brighten up when hearing Christi's heartfelt words of love to him.

"Christi has made me the happiest man on Earth," Jack stated proudly.

"And she wants you to know that when it is your time to be in spirit, she will make you the happiest man in Heaven."

Again feeling the love from Christi as she said these tender words to Jack made me tear up as well.

"Christi does have one request though, Jack," I told him.

"Anything."

"*Christi still wants to go on that cruise.*"

"*She does?*" he asked.

"*Of course! She says that you both were looking forward to it and she still is! Christi is telling me that you know for sure now that she will be with you and enjoying all of the adventures that you two had been planning. So go ahead, book a cruise, so you both can have a good time.*"

Jack responded, excitedly, "*Okay, I will then. If that is what Christi wants, I will be happy to do it!*"

"*Christi says you owe her that dance on the deck under the moonlight.*"

Jack smiled from ear to ear. "*We promised each other a waltz under the stars, just the two of us.*"

"*Keep that promise,*" *I told him.*

"*I will,*" *Jack affirmed, with new determination.*

———

Jack emailed my office a month or so later and sent a picture of him standing onboard a cruise ship, taking the trip that he and Christi had been planning. It was nice to see a big smile on Jack's face. In the photo, a large orb of light appeared on the right side of Jack. We knew this was also Christi in the picture, having the time of her life with the man she will love for all eternity.

Linking with Spirit

Connections and signs can and will happen to a person with little to no effort involved. But if you would like to make a stronger connection with a loved one in spirit, you can do it through meditation.

Yes, I will be honest; meditation can be difficult for most people. But I have learned from Patrick, it is all in how you approach it! (A secret about Patrick is that when he first started to develop his gift, he too had to learn how to meditate ... and hated it! But he discovered through trial and error his own personal way to meditate and let's just say it worked out pretty well for him!)

Meditation only means learning how to quiet your mind and focus. Believe it or not, you put yourself in a meditative state every day. From driving a car, to even doing chores around the house, activities take thought and focus, because you are meditating on them. This is also why, when you are doing these actions, you will notice connections from loved ones in spirit. I know that when I am cooking I connect with many of the ladies of my family. They are all excellent cooks and bakers and cooking brings us all together. Many times when I am just about to put a cake or other dish in the oven, a left-out ingredient will "pop" into my head and I will save the dish just in time. It is my heavenly help communicating with me. I am in a meditative state, which means I am focused and can connect with them easier. Patrick says that cooking is the best time for me to meditate…hmmm, I think he's just hungry!

But the next form of meditating I will now address does require you to stop doing your daily activities and take a few minutes to connect with your loved ones in spirit.

To do this, all you need to do is to sit down for five or ten minutes initially and focus on having a conversation with your loved one. While you are sitting there, imagine your loved one sitting beside you. When this vision becomes clear, start up a conversation with them, but the key is to listen to what they are saying to you. As you are conversing with your loved one in spirit, you may even be surprised by feeling their love for you as well!

Remember, there is no time limit when reconnecting. This is something you may notice right away, or slowly, as it becomes apparent. But your loved ones in spirit are always connected to you through their love…and that is what really counts!

PART FIVE

❦

ROMANTIC
MEDITATIONS

Many times when you think back on the past memories you have of a person you love, you will experience feelings of joy, gratitude, and excitement.

But why just stop at past memories, why not make new ones?

The following pages will help you create new memories with a loved one, whether they are with you in spirit or with you in this physical realm.

18. New Journeys

――――

What better way to make a connection with a loved one than to take a trip and experience new surroundings, making wonderful memories with the one you love.

The purpose of these meditations you are about to read is for you and your loved one to escape to a beautiful location and enjoy each other's company while also exploring the love you share in mind, body, and soul.

As you read the following stories, imagine yourself and your loved one on these memorable trips. If a paragraph ends with ..., I suggest that you close your eyes for a few minutes and picture yourself experiencing what you have just read.

During this time, ask yourself...

What are the sights and the sounds you are seeing and hearing in your mind?

What are the feelings you have about the place you are visiting?

How is the other person reacting on this journey with you?

What messages and feelings are you receiving from your loved one?

You can use these meditations if your loved one is still with you physically, or if they are in spirit…don't be surprised if you feel a special connection with them as you take these excursions together!

19. Southern Comfort

You and your loved one decide this would be a good time to get away. Packing your overnight bags, you zip them up, check the house to make sure every appliance is off, and lock the door. Getting in the car, you and your lover are both excited about what lies ahead. You hit the road and impulsively decide to drive to destinations unknown. It doesn't really matter where you go just as long as you two are together. Taking a deep breath, you find the anticipation of where this journey will lead leaves you feeling excited and energized.

As you drive down the highway, you notice that the trees on the side of the road start to become more plentiful and lush. And even though you don't know where both of you are heading, you will know when the feeling is right.

Sign after sign dots the highway, advertising vacations spots and relaxing resorts. But nothing looks right, that is until when you see a small sign suggesting a Bed and Breakfast Inn several miles off the highway. You both agree that this looks like where you need to head and decide to take the next exit and visit this quaint southern town ...

———————

You call the B&B as you are driving around the wooded curves to see if there is a room available for you. The clerk on the other end of the phone sounds pleasant and seems to be eager for you to try their hospitality, telling you he has a room he knows you are going to love.

The weather is gorgeous and as you drive around the streets of this old town you spot the B&B and you both agree that you made the right decision. The facility is a lovely, quaint house from the 1800s. Painted yellow, it has green shutters and a large front porch. Rocking chairs line the porch while a long white railing frames the house.

As you both exit the car, you walk up the steps leading to the door and notice an older woman sitting in a rocking chair. She smiles at you and you return the smile as you head inside. When you enter the B&B, you notice that the entrance hall is small, but decorated in a grand style. An antique table sits in the middle of the room with a miniature palm tree in a cloisonné pot sitting atop it.

A young man at the front desk smiles and waves you in. The clerk has a very strong southern accent and asks if you were the one who called to reserve the room. You acknowledge that you were, and he checks you in, giving you the keys to your retreat...

————

You both go up the grand dark wooden staircase, which is topped off by a large stained-glass window. The sun is shining through this window and a prism of colors from the glass seems to dance on the landing. You feel bathed in this extraordinary light show and the energy of the sun.

Finding your room and unlocking the heavy wooden door, you swing it open to find a beautifully decorated room. A white fireplace with a large wooden mantel is the centerpiece. It has brass candlesticks on each end and a portrait of a young girl from an era long ago hangs in the center.

A welcome basket of fruit and cookies greets you on the table, along with a bottle of wine. You set your luggage on the bed and as you start to unpack, you notice a lovely, intricately carved armoire in the corner. You take out your belongings and place them in this beautiful old piece of furniture.

The king-size canopy bed looks inviting as you both just fall onto the crisp white duvet of the featherbed. Sinking into what feels like a cloud you both sigh and turn to each other. You don't even feel like getting up, and start to talk...

———

After relaxing for a time, you both get your second wind and decide to explore the town. Going back down the stairs, you notice several other people checking in and start to sense the happy feeling that fills this house. Opening the screen door and stepping onto the front porch, you notice the older lady that was there when you checked in has been joined by her husband. A handsome man in his eighties, he is offering his love a frosted glass of iced tea. They make a cute couple and you both smile as you leave the B&B.

The sidewalk gives way to old cobblestone pathways. A group of people are walking on the other side of the tree-lined streets. As you pass a man on a bike, he smiles but seems to be concentrating on where he is going. As you continue on, you both look up and notice the bright blue sky is filled with huge white clouds. You each try to name what the biggest cloud looks like to you. Is it an elephant or a giraffe? But the clouds soon melt away as you continue your journey with the late afternoon sun shining down, filtering through the trees. The light from the leaves makes shimmering patterns on the walkways as if the leaves are falling and swirling on the ground...

———

Passing a small coffee shop, you both decide to stop for some refreshments. This building looks as if it had been an old garage in the 1940s, with little white tables and chairs dotting the outside veranda. Although the inside of the café looks inviting, the day is just too beautiful to be inside and you decide to sit outside.

As you sit and relax, you look around and notice baskets filled with trailing red begonias and ivy that hang from several posts. A waitress emerges from the inside, smiling at you both, and takes your order. When she leaves, you start to converse...

———

As you finish your beverages, the waitress comes to you and suggests that you must see the city parks. Feeling renewed and ready to go, you both decide to take her suggestion and continue on to the city square.

You come upon a large park filled with several brick-lined paths and fountains. Four amazingly large oak trees surround the largest fountain in the middle of the square. The Spanish moss drips from each branch as if placed there carefully by a world-class decorator. It is magnificent in its beauty and grace. A breeze begins to blow, cool at first, then warmer air envelops you both. The moss sways in unison back and forth. Hypnotic in its rhythm, it seems to keep time to the sounds of the square. Squirrels roam the park and jump from bench to bench, chattering with each other as if they were commenting on the beauty of their surroundings as well. The fountain flows from the side of the stone bowl into the larger bowl underneath. Two gray doves sit atop and coo. You are not the only lovers here today…

———

The daylight grows short and you decide to start back to your hotel to change for dinner. Someone had mentioned to you at the hotel that the riverfront is a must see. So on the way back to the B&B, you take a side street that leads to the riverfront.

Old buildings line the street and gas lamps light the way. The steps that lead down to the river are huge blocks of stone that once were ballasts for the old sailing ships that used to come to this city. The water glistens with the colors of the sunset as the bright orange ball of light, the setting sun slips behind the horizon. A tug boat toots its horn as it passes a larger ship and it sounds like a goose honking out loud. You both laugh at the sound and watch the little tug boat make its way past larger boats, acting as if this river belonged to her. The streets grow darker, illuminated with the centuries-old lamps and the street begins to fill up quickly. The day gives way to the night and a different group of people fill the streets.

Walking back the short distance to your B&B, you have arranged a romantic dinner in your room by the fireplace. You both freshen up and dress in your evening clothes. After all, this is a special event, just for the two of you. The fireplace is aglow with a romantic fire that has been lit for you. A small mahogany table has been placed in your room in front of the fireplace. The table is set beautifully. A white tablecloth and antique ladder-back chairs frame the gorgeous table setting. Fine silverware from the 1800s sits atop blue-and-white bone china plates. Sparkling crystal glasses glisten, reflecting the flames of the roaring fire. You both sit down and soak in the atmosphere. There will be no rushed evening tonight; you have all the time you need to enjoy this setting. Lace curtains soften the lights of the street below where the shadows of people rushing to one place or another filter through.

Filling your glasses, you toast each other and this wonderful night. The crystal clinks with an almost musical sound. You look into each other's eyes as you sip your beverage. A feast has been prepared for you and you don't know where to begin. Between the appetizer and the main course, you don't think you can even eat another bite; that is, until you see the dessert, a seven-layer red velvet cake for which the B&B is famous. The food was wonderful and the dessert is even better. Sharing it with each other, you wipe the whipped cream off each other's noses and laugh …

————

Finishing this marvelous meal, you decide to sit on your private balcony that faces the courtyard in the back. The black wrought-iron bars of the balcony fade into the darkness of the night and it's almost as if you are floating among the trees that fill the courtyard.

The half moon fills the yard with subdued blue light, reflecting off the small pond below. Stars fill the night sky and the breeze that was warmed by the sun today now blows cooler. Chilled, you wrap your arms around each other, taking in this nighttime scene. Reflecting on all the day's events, you can almost feel the other person's thoughts.

It's time to come in from the night air and think back, to reflect on this wonderful day's events. What an adventure you have had! You turn down the fluffy white comforter and you both rest your head on the oversized down pillows. As you get closer, nestling next to each other, you smile, relax, and enjoy one another's love.

20. Picnic Adventure

───────

The sun filters through the soft white sheers of the big bay window as a gentle breeze lifts them quietly off the floor. A sweet smell fills the air and you look to see what could be making such a heavenly scent. You open the side window and see a column of color, a bright purple staff of morning glories hiding the honeysuckle vine that wraps around the fence near the porch. It beckons you to come outside today. You decide to enjoy this glorious day with your love by exploring the outdoors and taking a picnic lunch for the two of you.

Going into the kitchen you find a brown wicker basket sitting on the top shelf of the cupboard in the corner of the kitchen. Looking around, you spot that bottle of wine you have been saving for a special occasion. You pack the basket with the wine and several other goodies. Through the open window in the kitchen you hear the melodious chirping of a songbird. Parting the red-checkered curtains, you look out into the yard. A squirrel is attempting to finish up the last of the birdseed you threw down this morning, as a cat stretches and falls back to sleep on the swing under the oak tree. Taking the basket, you head to the front door, but remember you forgot the blanket for the picnic. You quickly open the linen closet and pull out the blanket from the top shelf. Packing it into the basket, you again head out the door with your loved one. The screen door creaks as you open it as if to say goodbye...

———

The front porch is dotted with different colors on one side as you have been planting miniature roses in terra cotta pots. Some of the pots even boast a green patina from the years of use, and their age just adds to their lustrous beauty.

Hand in hand with your love, you set out for the distant field that lies ahead. Stepping off the porch, you both breathe in the perfumed aroma of the honeysuckle and the brisk fresh air. It fills your lungs and you now are able to experience this wonderful day that a few minutes ago was only a view you glimpsed from inside the house. You feel invigorated as the two of you stroll together down the gray slate walkway. Stopping, you notice a tiny green frog has jumped onto the slate. He is so small, and yet you would swear he smiled at you as you stepped over him on your way to the meadow...

———

Woods lie just ahead that you must cross first before you reach the meadow, where you plan to devour the food and drink in the basket. Walking through all of the beautiful tall trees, you begin to pick up the sound of water. As you head toward the gurgling sound, the path you take leads you to a stream that is lined with wondrous silver maple trees. The silvery leaves glisten as they shimmer in the breeze and make the water in the stream seem to hold diamonds floating on top when the filtered sunlight plays over it. Careful not to slip, you grab the hand of your partner and jump to the other side of the stream and continue on your journey.

As you start making your way out of the woods, you come across some hills where just beyond lies the meadow. The grass on the hills is tall and sways in the wind as if an invisible hand were brushing it side to side. You stop to marvel at the light changing the color of the hills from green to almost a pale yellow as the clouds float past the sun. This too would be a perfect spot for the picnic but alas, the grass is too tall. You remember the meadow as one of the most perfect spots you have ever come across and decide to continue on. As you begin to climb one of the hills, the grass invigorates you; you feel like a child again. Carefree, you look at each other and the race is on to see who can reach the top of the hill first. Giggling, you run hard and fast, trying to catch your breath. The grass brushes your legs with a soft caress as you go faster and faster. Stopping just short of the very top, you both look at each other and laugh—it was a tie…

———

Climbing to the top of the grassy knoll, you look down and see the meadow. There it lies in splendor. From this distance it appears as a handmade quilt with small squares of yellows, purples, and pinks. As you make your way down from the hill, the squares of color become large areas of wildflowers, seemingly untouched by anyone, nestled in this meadow for you alone to enjoy. Finally reaching the bottom you are now in this beautiful valley. As you are walking through these flowers the sweet aroma mixed in with the warmth of the sun is energizing you both. You can't stop yourself, and you pick several from each area. The yellow ones are sunflowers with long green stems, orange petals, and dark seed-filled centers. Just as you are about to break the stem of one, a yellow and black bumblebee flies off the flower. No worries as he has many more to explore before his day is done. You take a few sunflowers and continue on. The purple flowers are in bunches closer to the ground and you have to pull them up carefully. Each multilayered flower has several different amethyst hues and the petals have the texture of velvet. Next you come across the pink ones. These are delicate, almost like tiny orchids. Thin, tiny stems that bend gracefully to the whim of the wind. Gathering them all up together, you have a beautiful floral bouquet and you know that it will be the perfect centerpiece of the picnic lunch.

When you come across a clearing, you decide it is time to take out the blanket that you had packed for this adventure. In the middle of the meadow is a majestic old oak tree. It appears to be three trees that have grown together. At one time this tree would have seemed to touch the sky, but many years have gone by and its once proud limbs that stretched out forever now are weathered and broken by storms and age. A large limb from the oak tree that fell years ago sits under the tree and will make a comfortable bench for the two of you. Deciding this is the spot for you, you unfurl the blanket and it softly rests on the grass below. You lay your flower bouquet in the center and open the basket. You are both famished; all this fresh air and exercise has made you hungry...

———

You take out several cheeses and arrange them on a plate along with crackers and grapes. One cheese is pale in color and soft in texture. It is almost sweet, which complements the taste of the salty cracker. The other cheese is dark yellow, almost orange in color, and is more brittle. It has a salty taste and goes well with the grapes you brought along. After pouring the delicious wine, you raise a toast to the day and this unexpected but exciting adventure. You finish with two petit fours for dessert. They are diamond-shaped little cakes decorated with chocolate icing and two delicate pink flowers in the middle. When you bite into one, the chocolate that surrounds the cake cracks to release its sweetness, and the moist cake inside adds its flavor. Sweet strawberry filling drips out of the cake and some falls on your chin. You wipe it away and lick your fingers. This is a feast fit for a king, or at least a really good picnic.

Lying back on the blanket, you both look up at the sky. The white clouds that once dotted the bright blue sky have become larger. They are almost like mountains of fluffy cotton on the edge of a blue ocean. Taking a moment, you both reflect on life and love...

———

In the distance you hear a slight rumble. While lying there, you can almost feel the earth tremble. As the sound draws closer you notice what once was a blue sky is now turning gray. The white clouds that filled the sky are now dark gray, swirling closer to the fading sun. The rumbling sound is closer and a few drops of rain hit your face. A loud clap of thunder resounds overhead and you both gather the blanket and basket and run for cover.

Seeking shelter in the storm, you see a small, rundown one-room cabin that seems to have been abandoned years ago. With the rain pouring now, you both run toward the cabin and hesitantly push open the door. A few of the wooden slats of the door are missing and it swings open, tilting to one side as a hinge gives way. The roof and floor seem stable and you decide to wait out the storm here. Shaking the rain off the blanket, you sit on the floor and wrap yourself in the warm wool. A chill has overtaken you from your wet clothing, but the blanket and snuggle with your loved one will warm you up soon enough…

———

Looking around you see a few signs of life from the past. A few old pots and pans sit on the small wooden table in the center of the room. Other than that, there is no furniture except a small broken ladder-back chair on its side near the window. Cobwebs hang in the corners and dust covers everything there. Looking through the cracked glass of what was once the front window, you see the rain descending in sheets outside. You feel lucky to have found this refuge; otherwise, you both would have been drenched. Remembering that you still have the basket, you take out two ruby-red apples that you have been saving for the walk home. This is the perfect time to share them. The bite is crisp and their taste is so sweet. Some of the juice is running down your neck and your partner wipes it off. This place isn't so bad after all. Looking out again, you notice the top of a window flowerbox on the outside of the broken window and a small, rusty, garden hand-shovel left there. At one time, someone who lived here must have loved flowers. This place holds a pleasant energy and you can imagine some sweet older lady living out her days watching the beautiful meadow and taking care of her beds of cultivated flowers…

———

Lost in your thoughts, you feel the warmth of sunlight hitting your arm from a crack in the door. The rain has stopped and the sun is shining bright again.

You brush yourselves off and gather your possessions. Silently thanking this cabin for its shelter, you open the creaking door and decide it's time to go home.

While walking through the rain-soaked meadow, back over the tall grass hills and through the woods, you contemplate all the wonderful events of the day and all the new memories you have made.

21. Winter Cabin

———

It's a chilly, blustery day and work for the week is done. You and your love are sitting on the porch sipping the last drops of morning coffee as you look out at the tips of the mountains far off in the distance. Thinking about a perfect getaway, you look at each other and decide to visit your cabin, nestled in those far-off mountains.

———

Packing doesn't take long as you keep all the essentials there already. You check the weather and there is a chance of snow, but all the better, as you just want to be alone with each other. Grabbing your coats, you head out the door and start this winter adventure...

———

Driving up to your cabin, deep in the woods, you start to relax. Leaving all your cares behind, you find the scenery takes your breath away. The well-traveled roads of the city start to empty as the cars and their passengers have other destinations in mind. You pass fields that were once lush and vibrant with tall stalks of corn swaying in the summer winds. Only the stumps of the stalks now remain as the farmers harvested the corn months ago. Some farmers have planted winter wheat and the green fields seem to tease the land as if spring has arrived. Cows in the field enjoy the sun while it gives them warmth. You notice a small calf standing close to his mother as it yearns for her love and protection. Driving on, you notice that the houses are less and less frequent and the mountains draw nearer.

————

You see the small grocery store at the base of the mountain. It's a cute white clapboard building with a green tin roof, and its age shows that it has been there for many decades. As you open the creaky old screen door, an older gentleman smiles from behind the register on the well-worn wooden counter. The whole atmosphere is as if you have walked into a Norman Rockwell painting. A sad-eyed black-and-white beagle sits near the feet of the clerk and they both seem to be listening to the radio. You notice that the clerk is eating peanut butter cookies and slips his dog a bite every now and then.

———

You gather your perishables and a few other goodies and check out. This kindly old gentleman chats with you about the events of the day and seems pleased to have your company. As he bags the groceries in the paper bag and slides it over the counter to you, he reminds you that this is the last stop and says to make sure you take everything you need in case of inclement weather. He "feels" a storm a brewing in his bones and says to hurry up the mountain before she hits. Leaving the store you feel as if you've seen an old friend from long ago...

———

The sun is beginning to set and you both decide to pull-over on the side of the road to take in the magnificent view. What were once green mountains are now only speckled with the green of pine trees and other evergreens, as the brown trunks and limbs of the once robust oak trees and sycamores line the road. On the horizon, the sun is setting like a blazing red ball. Gently slipping behind the tops of the mountains, it quietly sets; only a pink halo remains. Night begins to fall and stars start to sparkle in the twilight sky.

———

You stand in awe of nature's majesty, taking a deep breath as your lungs fill with the cold, crisp air. Breathing out all of your problems and tensions, you both feel so refreshed.

———

Getting back in your car, you continue onward, winding through these picturesque mountain roads, heading toward your cabin retreat. It's been your refuge, your reflective spot where worries, problems, and tensions disappear…

———

You both become excited when you see the log cabin appear in front of you. Everything looks great and as you step onto the large front porch, you open the shutters that protected the picture window until you returned. Before entering your log retreat you check for firewood as snow is predicted later in the evening. A large stack sits next to the rocking chairs just as you left it on your last visit.

———

Upon unlocking the door, you detect the sweet smell of cinnamon filling the air as a large jar candle has been left open on the coffee table near the door. The table is a project that you both embarked on several visits ago. You made it from a white birch tree that was uprooted in a

storm awhile back. The beautiful peeling white bark uncovers the pale yellow wood underneath and frames the
glass top perfectly. A large green, three-cushion sofa rests
in front of the table. It looks so inviting that you both decide to just relax on the cushy pillows and take a moment
to adjust to the change of scene. A large patchwork quilt
hangs on the wall near the stone fireplace. Feeling a chill
in the air, you know that this respite is short lived and you
both have work to do …

———

After unpacking the car, you stack some logs in the fireplace. Taking a match from the holder on the mantle,
you light the kindling underneath the logs. A small, glow-
ing red flame starts to dance until it grows and engulfs
all the logs. The chill of the cabin begins to give way to
the warmth of the crackling fire.

———

Both of you are feeling hungry now and you heat up some
beef stew and biscuits that you bought at the grocery store
at the bottom of the mountain. The faucet squeaks and
gurgles from not being used, like the sounds of someone
waking after sleeping for too long. The cold spring water
soon flows from the tap and the water is on the stove for
hot tea.

––––––––

You take a checkered tablecloth from the cabinet near the sink and shake it out before spreading it to cover the small dining table in the kitchen. It seems to suit the table as if it were hugging an old friend. The blue-and-white dishes add such a cheery feel to the dinner. The stew smells delicious as the aroma fills the cabin. The brown gravy from the stew is thick and rich as it soaks the large chunks of potatoes and beef. You can't help but dunk the butter biscuits in the bowl of stew to savor the salty warm taste ...

––––––––

After dinner you decide to sit near the fire with hot tea and buttery shortbread.

While sitting at the hearth, you feel the heat from the crackling fire and it warms you both as you hold each other in a gentle embrace. The fire has many colors in the dancing flames. You notice the blue at the base near the logs that changes to a brilliant yellow, orange, and red. It is almost a reflection of the multi-hued sunset that greeted the oncoming night at the lookout a few hours ago.

––––––––

A soft green light shining on the wall catches your eye. Curious, you follow the source to see that the first beams of moonlight have caught the reflective prisms of a green crystal vase that rests on the window ledge.

———

In the mood for a short outing, you decide to take a walk outside as the full moon has now risen. Grabbing your sweaters, you both step outside onto the front porch.

———

The moonlight has illuminated everything with a pale blue shimmer. Even the lake below seems to sparkle like bits of sapphires as the gentle breeze ripples the water. Everything has been kissed by the moonlight as it seems to purify everything it touches. The light breeze begins to pick up now. The tops of the tall pines sway in unison as small clouds seem to dance around the full moon. A cold chill is in the air and you feel that snow is on its way. Gathering more firewood, you step back in and stack it near the fireplace...

———

Your outdoor adventure has chilled you both and you decide that nothing would be better now than some steaming hot chocolate. Heating the milk, you shave some dark chocolate from a block of chocolate kept in the fridge.

You add it slowly to the milk so as to not burn the delicate ingredients. The once-white milk turns darker with each stir and the air soon fills with its sweet aroma. You finish this delightful drink by dropping a few small marshmallows in the cup. You watch them melt to create a creamy delight as you take the hot mugs of goodness to the sofa.

————

A soft, russet-colored cashmere throw lays across the back of the sofa and you wrap it around you both. Sipping the hot chocolate fills you with warmth and comfort. You nestle closer to each other and look out through the big picture window.

————

The bright full moon has dimmed as clouds cover the sky. You then see the first few flakes of snow begin to fall. Lightly at first, the flakes become bigger and fall faster. You can see the railing on the front porch and the branches of the closest trees start to turn white. What a wonderful time to be snowed in with the one you love!

————

The fire starts to die down and you get up to put on more logs. The red-hot embers fall to the bottom of the fireplace as the new large logs are placed on top. Standing at the window, you watch the snowflakes cover the ground with a white blanket of new snow. A sense of quiet stills the air. It seems you can almost hear each gentle flake falling and quietly touching the ground. You sit back, enjoy the fire, and reflect on the time you're having together.

What a wonderful experience!

22. LIGHTHOUSE VISIT

———

It's a great day for an unexpected adventure for you and the one you love. You have been driving the scenic coast for miles and finally reach your destination. You park and walk to a weathered old dock that seems to be home to seagulls and fishermen. Large pillars, cracked from the sun and wind, are tied taut with large bands of rope. The birds rest on the top of each pillar, looking at the people walking below as if they are the show. As you step onto the dock, you see the ferry that you have been awaiting. It's still a bit far off, so you relax on a bench nearby. It's a wonderful sunny, warm day and as you both breathe in the salt air from the sea, you are spellbound by the simple beauty of the day-to-day life of the small coastal town.

Watching the boat come closer and closer, you start to make your way down a small hill to the ferry, which has now just docked. The deck hands secure the vessel to the landing like clockwork and open the ferry to take on passengers. Once aboard, you climb the tiny metal steps to the top deck. The old boat's many coats of white paint have peeled with age and the sea air. There are not many passengers onboard and you are the only ones on the top deck. As you look out in the distance, you can see for miles from your vantage point, and it seems as if the rippling water meets and touches the crisp blue sky.

As your adventure continues, in the near distance you see your final destination appear, a small beachfront that lies ahead. At first it seems like just a small deserted strip of land, but as you get closer, you can see the pristine beach that beckons adventurous travelers like the two of you ...

———

Once the ferry nears the shore, the captain barks orders to the men below and they gear up to secure the boat when she docks. You both climb down the tight set of steps to the deck below. The boat jolts as it bounces off the pier, where tires tied to posts keep it from crashing into the dock. The deck hands ask you to watch your step as you go up onto the waiting ramp. After climbing up, then down, you see the beach at your feet.

The sand feels warm with the afternoon sun shining down on it. It's surprisingly soft, and with each footstep it separates your toes as you sink into it. The sky is bright blue with only a few thin white clouds on the horizon, as you walk hand in hand on the shore where the water meets the sand. The waves from the ocean are rolling in gently and as they finally reach your feet, you both jump back a little and laugh as the cool water is a surprise. Your feet begin sinking in the sand as it gets wet with each wave that rolls on top of it. White foam tickles your feet each time the water is drawn back into the ocean. Beautiful shells that were not there before appear when the water slips back and you notice a particular small, smooth white shell and decide to pick it up. As you wipe off the sand from the shell, you see it has a bright yellow dot in the center of it. You compose a story of this special one-of-kind shell that tells it is a rare gem of the sea, and your partner adds to the tale as well. You decide to keep this treasured memory and place the shell in your pocket as a reminder of this day. You embrace each other as the world's cares seem to melt into the ocean with each receding wave.

You both walk farther down to what seems to be a deserted beach, when you see a couple of people coming toward you in the distance. As you continue walking, and the couple is making their way closer to you, you are able to discern that they are an older couple. The woman carries a small dog in her arms. As you pass each other, you exchange pleasantries and wish them a good day and when you look back, you notice they kiss each other, and the love they have for each other is palpable...

———

As you continue your walk, you start to notice that the landscape is becoming rocky and even the once gentle waves are now crashing on the rocks. You are now on the other side of the beach, which is not visible from the ferry. As you look around, it seems to be uninhabited, and as you both set out to continue your adventure, suddenly you see a lighthouse up in the distance. You decide to visit it.

As you approach the lighthouse, you notice its faded black stripes that wrap around the building and the glass on top shines from the reflected sunlight. It stands above the rocks defiantly, as if to warn of all danger from the sea. You also spot a small cottage attached to the main structure and are determined to get a closer look. As you look around, you see a small path hidden by a white picket fence that winds its way to the top of the small hill on which the lighthouse sits. Your partner grabs your hand and you make your way up. The grass is tall and thick and sways to and fro with the breeze from the sea. After reaching the top of this hill, you catch your breath and look up. The lighthouse that appeared to be small from below is now a massive, striped column that seems to stretch to the top of the sky. You both squint as the sun shines bright from above. You approach the cottage. It's small and white-washed, built of the same white bricks that make up the lighthouse, and dwarfed by that massive structure next to it. Purple grass lines the foundation of the structure and its color pops against the bold white background of the cottage. A few broken pieces of gray slate suffice for a walkway and you walk toward the front door.

There seems to be no bell to ring and so you knock on the front door. No one answers. Not wanting to waste an opportunity, you peek in the cottage windows. Although your partner wants you to leave, you insist that you just want to take a quick look inside ...

———

As you peer in, you notice the old-fashioned pull shades with a string and a ring pull covering the top half of the front window. Farther in, you see a small kitchen with a tiny sink and stove. A small wooden table has two chairs, with one pulled out as if someone had just been there. A black-speckled enamel coffee pot sits on the stove and one cup sits on the sink beside it. Your partner tells you to hurry before someone catches you both!

But just as you are about to turn around to leave, a man's low voice breaks the silence. "Can I help you?" he says in a stern tone. Shaken, you catch your breath and try to explain that you were just out and about, and you fumble with the reasoning behind your spying on someone else's house. The man starts to frown at you both with an uncomfortable pause following, and then he laughs out loud.

Nervously, you both laugh along with him and he then introduces himself as the lighthouse keeper. He tells you that every now and then he gets unexpected visitors brought by the ferry and is happy to have the company. You are both so relieved that he understands why you were peeking in the cottage and continue to laugh at yourselves. The keeper invites you into the lighthouse for a closer look…

———

You and your love go with him through a small door located at the bottom of the structure. Once inside, you see a massive winding iron staircase that leads to the very top of the lighthouse, and the keeper insists that a short tour is in order. As you start climbing the long stairs, the caretaker gives you the history of the lighthouse and lists all the caretakers that have come before him. He seems genuinely pleased to have company as he spins his yarns of the sea. He stops halfway at a landing where a small four-pane window lets in the light of day. Looking out, he points to the end of an outcropping of large jagged boulders and tells you of a ship that ran aground a hundred years ago in that very spot. You take your partner's hand as he speaks of the shipwreck that had no survivors and yet there seem to be signs from those who perished that they remain present there to this day. After midnight when the moon is dark, he explains, you can see strange lights floating around those very rocks. He himself has seen the lights. You squeeze your love's hand tightly and tell the lighthouse keeper that you do not believe in ghosts. He smiles with a half grin and assures you that if you stayed the night, you would.

As you continue on with the tour, the keeper takes you both to the top of the lighthouse where a large light is surrounded by a prism of glass. It's massive up close and the view is absolutely breathtaking as you take a moment to breathe it all in.

After chatting a few more minutes with the keeper, you all notice that the sun is going to set soon and he says he must get going. You thank him for his kindness and ask if you can visit him again. He says he's happy that you enjoyed yourselves and insists you both come back soon, promising the coffee will be hot next time…

———

You go down the winding path, back through the tall grass and white fence to find yourselves once again on the sandy beach. The wind seems colder now and your walk back is faster than the one up. The last ferry will leave later that evening so you decide to find the perfect place on the beach to relax and watch the sunset. The once-blue sky is now changing to gray and lavender tones, and the sun that was once golden and bright in the sky now slips into the far horizon. As the sun sets, it seems to become larger and closer, and as you both snuggle close to one another, the sun gives way to night.

Hugging each other tighter, you both gaze at the beautiful night sky. Only a single bright twinkling light shines overhead and you both say "make a wish" to each other and laugh. It seems that your wishes have come true already. You feel like the two of you could talk for hours as the sky starts to fill with stars. You name the constellations and even make up some because the words just sound good. The sound of the ocean has grown softer at the calming of the sea, as the stars give way to the rising moon. It is only a sliver of silver, but its light shines down on you both.

The horn of the approaching ferry signals the end of this amazing day. Walking to the dock, you look around one more time as the moonlight kisses the sand and water. You feel closer to each other than you ever have and hold each other tight as the sea breeze wraps around your bodies.

In Closing

The start of this book began with the definition of love, but really, can anyone describe what love is in words?

Love is more than just a noun, a verb, or even an emotion; love is the true essence of who we are as human beings, and as spirits. Love is a gift that can transform who we are, how we act, and how we perceive this world in which we live. It is the core and the essence of all that is good. It is a gift we are able to give to others, but also one we must remember to give to ourselves as well.

Life is love and love is life, and that is what life is all about … here and in spirit.

The love bond between you and your loved ones in spirit is eternal. It is important to continue moving forward, living this life and recognizing your own connections, knowing that those in spirit are and will always be with you, loving you as you love them.

Throughout the pages of this book amazing love stories have unfolded within the many readings shared. Some to let their loves know that their path on this earth includes their being open for new relationships so that they may share their strong gift of love with others. Some to let their loves know that their journey together will continue even though one is in spirit, making new memories for each other along the way. The one constant is the great love shared and the truth that love never dies. Each of us have a special journey that we must see to completion. It can seem daunting when a partner who has been by your side has passed on and now you feel you must face this journey alone. The purpose of this book is to show that not only are you not alone but your love that has carried you through this life so far will indeed continue.

In trying to help you connect with yourself and your loved one, the tools presented in the past chapters will help lead you to having stronger bonds with each other. Whether you start off with something so simple yet so poignant as writing love letters to each other, or recognizing the memory sparks that take you back to special places, your relationship with your loved one can continue and assist you in living life to the fullest.

The meditations in this book give you the opportunity to experience new surroundings, new journeys together. By taking the time to travel in your mind or to really "travel" with your loved one, whether present or in spirit, you can connect and start new paths together!

Like life, love has daily challenges and takes work, but by using love to not only ground your soul but to feed it you will strengthen the bond, the relationship you have, and move forward through this life with joy.

Both Kathy and I feel blessed by experiencing the love of those who have shared their stories in this book, along with the countless others we have met through our work along the way. As stated in the beginning of this book, "Everyone has a story," and this includes you!

Always remember, your life, your love, and "your story" is as important in this world as anyone else's . . . and of that, you can be sure.

To Write the Authors

If you wish to contact the authors or would like more information about this book, please write to the author in care of Llewellyn Worldwide, and we will forward your request. Llewellyn Worldwide cannot guarantee that every letter written to the author can be answered, but all will be forwarded. Please write to:

Patrick and Kathleen Mathews
⅟ Llewellyn Worldwide
2143 Wooddale Drive
Woodbury, MN 55125-2989

Please enclose a self-addressed stamped envelope for reply, or $1.00 to cover costs. If outside the USA, enclose an international postal reply coupon.

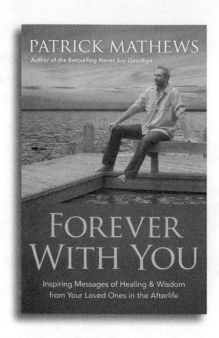

PATRICK MATHEWS
Author of the Bestselling *Never Say Goodbye*

FOREVER
WITH YOU

Inspiring Messages of Healing & Wisdom
from Your Loved Ones in the Afterlife

Forever With You
Inspiring Messages of Healing & Wisdom from your Loved Ones in the Afterlife
PATRICK MATHEWS

After the phenomenal success of *Never Say Goodbye,* Patrick Mathews became one of the most recognized mediums in the country. *Forever With You* invites us back for a closer look at his fascinating life as a spirit communicator and all he's learned.

These vivid and unforgettable stories help us understand what it's like to talk to spirits, how our loved ones have—and haven't—changed since crossing over, and how they continue to impact our lives. Answering questions only a medium can, Mathews offers insight into life's biggest mysteries—what happens when we pass into spirit, heaven and hell, God and angels, reincarnation, the purpose of our physical life, and more.

978-0-7387-2766-0, 240 pp., 5³⁄₁₆ x 8   **$15.95**

PATRICK MATHEWS

NEVER SAY GOODBYE

A Medium's Stories of
Connecting with Your Loved Ones

Never Say Goodbye
*A Medium's Stories of Connecting
with Your Loved Ones*
Patrick Mathews

"I'm a normal guy … I just speak to dead people."

When he was six years old, Patrick Mathews came face
to face with the spirit of his dead Uncle Edward. As an adult,
Mathews serves as a vessel of hope for those who wish to
communicate with their loved ones in spirit.

The stories Mathews tells of his life and the people he has
helped are humorous, heartwarming, and compelling. Part of
his gift is in showing the living that they can still recognize
and continue on-going relationships with the departed.

Mathews takes the reader on a roller coaster of emotional
stories, from the dead husband who stood by his wife's side
during her wedding to a new man, to the brazen spirit who
flashed her chest to get her point across. You will also learn
step-by-step methods for recognizing your own communica-
tions from beyond.

978-0-7387-0353-4, 216 pp., 6 x 9   **$15.95**

OVER 250,000
COPIES SOLD!

MICHAEL NEWTON, PH.D.

JOURNEY
OF
SOULS

CASE STUDIES OF
LIFE BETWEEN LIVES

Journey of Souls
Case Studies of Life Between Lives
Michael Newton, Ph.D.

This remarkable book uncovers—for the first time—the mystery of life in the spirit world after death on earth. Dr. Michael Newton, a hypnotherapist in private practice, has developed his own hypnosis technique to reach his subjects' hidden memories of the hereafter. The narrative is woven as a progressive travel log around the accounts of twenty-nine people who were placed in a state of super-consciousness. While in deep hypnosis, these subjects describe what has happened to them between their former reincarnations on earth. They reveal graphic details about how it feels to die, who meets us right after death, what the spirit world is really like, where we go and what we do as souls, and why we choose to come back in certain bodies.

After reading *Journey of Souls,* you will acquire a better understanding of the immortality of the human soul. Plus, you will meet day-to-day personal challenges with a greater sense of purpose as you begin to understand the reasons behind events in your own life.

978-1-567-18585-3, 288 pp., 6 x 9   **$16.95**

LOVE

and

INTUITION

A Psychic's Guide
to Creating Lasting Love

SHERRIE DILLARD

Love and Intuition
A Psychic's Guide to Creating Lasting Love
SHERRIE DILLARD

Love, by its very nature, is profoundly spiritual. Each of us can harness this transformative emotion by embracing our own natural intuition.

Building on the success of *Discover Your Psychic Type*, professional psychic Sherrie Dillard presents a life-changing paradigm based on the four love types. This unique book teaches you to develop your intuition to attract and sustain love, while enriching your relationship with your spouse or partner, friends, and yourself.

Once you find out your intuitive love type—emotional, spiritual, mental, or physical—you can then determine your spouse or partner's love type, and learn practical ways to strengthen your relationship and heighten intimacy.

978-0-7387-1555-1, 336 pp., 6 x 9   **$16.95**
